THE PATY FAMILY

Makers of Eighteenth-Century Bristol

GORDON PRIEST

First published in 2003 by Redcliffe Press Ltd,
81g Pembroke Road, Bristol BS8 3EA

Telephone 0117 9737207

Unless otherwise stated, the photographs are by the author.

Cover photograph by Stephen Morris, smc@freeuk.com

ISBN 1 900178 54 0

British Library Cataloguing-in-Publication-Data
A catalogue record for this book is available from the British Library.

Typeset by Datcon-Infotech, Frome, and printed by HSW Print, Tonypandy

CONTENTS

To Pam, Julia
and Olivia
with love

Introduction

The eighteenth-century architecture of Bristol was profoundly influenced by the Patys who emerged from a building family out of Somerset, probably from the Somerton area, in the early 1700s. In Bristol they had several workshops, run independently but working as a loose federation so that a Paty could call upon a brother or cousin for aid when it was needed. They were basically stone masons with special skill as carvers and sculptors. Their workshops were organised to the supply of carved, dressed stonework for Bristol builders, for whom they also supplied fireplaces, staircases, doors and panelling and, probably, windows. At the same time, they supplied marbles and slate and other special stones for floors and provided memorial tablets and tombs, for which they became well known throughout the West Country and further afield. It is not surprising that several of them became proficient architects and town planners.

Most of the recent studies of eighteenth-century Bristol buildings have suggested that there were three generations of Patys – a father, his sons and grandsons who were active between 1720 and 1800 – but I have been able to show that the first Paty, James(1) had a single, posthumous son who lived from 1747/8 to 1807, called James, whom I describe as James(3), and two nephews, Thomas and James(2), and their sons John(1), John(2) and William.

No previous attempt has been made to assemble biographical details or methodical lists of their works; nor had any qualitative judgement been attempted until Tim Mowl's assessment in *To Build the Second City* was published by Redcliffe Press in 1991. All the authors of books on Bristol's architectural history have agreed that the Patys were important yet information about them has been limited. Walter Ison attempted to set out the dynastic character of the family and how its influence spread through the whole of the eighteenth century in his *Georgian Buildings of Bristol* of 1952. This predated Rupert Gunnis's *Dictionary of British Sculptors, 1660–1850* and H.M. Colvin's *Biographical Dictionary of English Architects, 1660–1840* by one and two years respectively. They both repeated what Ison had stated, with one or two variations. No significant addition has been made since then.

Mr. Ison came closest to providing a proper context for the Paty clan and provided the springboard for this study. In five pages of text, he summarised the then known facts, which he had drawn from his searches in the City Archives (now Record) Office and elsewhere. In an introductory paragraph he said:

> The name of Paty figures so prominently in Bristol's eighteenth-century building history that its bearers deserve a detailed study beyond the scope of the present work. It is a matter of regret that evidence regarding some of them and their relationship one with the other is either inconclusive or altogether lacking. It is of course probable that widespread research would reveal more than is contained in the following.

Ison's proposed detailed study has now been attempted at last. Facts about the family nevertheless remain scarce. It is this that has put people off in the past and my own work has been spread over many years. I was first stimulated by Walter Ison's paragraph and this prompted me to encourage one of my students to write an essay about the Paty Copybook in the early 1960s which, in its turn, sent me in search of more information. It was soon apparent that there was not a great deal to discover and my work on the family was often pushed into the background of my life, in the teaching and practice of architecture and in conservation.

This is not, therefore, the result of forty years work but is a latter-day attempt to make sense of jottings and notes that have been accumulating and gathering dust. I have tried to describe this intriguing family without discovering any of the personal details that modern readers demand of a biographer. There are no portraits, no letters, no scandals, only some buildings, exquisite carving and other craftwork, some sculptured funeral monuments and a book of drawings to demonstrate their worth.

By re-examining the sources, I have exposed a few new fragments of information, found a few more Patys and, I think, made sense of the family tree. I have, I hope correctly, awarded Thomas Paty his 'ownership' of the design of Redland Chapel and thereby given him an important first building. For his son, William, I have raised the stakes on his first building, Christ Church, City, by suggesting that it is of national significance. Otherwise, I do not make many claims for the Patys. It may be true that we have so little information about them because there was little to leave. They were probably quiet, reserved and reasonably efficient in a society that had different values from our own. They were all marvellous craftsmen and some were brilliant architects too, content to be judged by what they left behind them.

They made eighteenth-century Bristol, and this was their monument.

Family Tree

No personal papers other than wills have been found to enliven the family story, nor have there been any useful biographical notes other than a few obituary notices. Virtually all the evidence has been collected from wills, business letters, civic minute books, estate documents, parish registers, electoral lists, drawings collections and so on. There are also some contemporary histories of Bristol, local guidebooks, newspaper reports and some later items that attest to the importance of the family in the development of Bristol.

The members of the family who contributed to Bristol's building history did not spring from a single branch but from two. There were uncles and cousins in the building trades, living in Bristol and operating independently, in separate workshops early in the 1700s and they continued to operate from them throughout the century. There were three and sometimes four family firms, working at the same time, providing essentially the same service.

The number of members of the family working early in the eighteenth century suggests fecundity as a characteristic which clearly did not survive, and early death among the males and small families were the norm in the second half of the century. Although it is now clear that a James Paty (a carver and gilder) survived in his workshop in Broadmead until 1807, the main connection with city development ceased in 1800.

When William Paty died in December 1800, the workshop, the architectural practice and the goodwill were sold to Mr Henry Wood, an architect and statuary from London. He lived in Bristol from then until his death in 1828, producing many memorial tablets and, probably, masonry details for buildings, but few recorded buildings. The main building tradition was to be continued by someone else: James Foster, who had been apprenticed to William Paty, set himself up in 1806 when he became a freeman of the city. The firm he started has the longest lineage of any architectural practice that I know of in Bristol, particularly if one includes Thomas and William Paty. James Foster soon became James Foster and Sons, then Foster and Okely, Foster and Wood (by this time, the Foster is a grandson of the first James and the Wood may have been a grandson of Henry Wood), then Foster, Wood and Awdry, a firm that was eventually purchased by Eustace Button. The practice continued as Eustace Button and later as Eustace Button and Partner under the direction of James Ackland until 1994. Mr. Button survived until 2001 when he died aged 101. He provided a direct link to the Patys. It may one day be necessary to extend this study to include the large volume of building created by this nineteenth- and twentieth-century practice with such important buildings as the original Colston Hall, Foster's Almshouses in Colston Street, the QEH School buildings, the original City Museum in Queen's Road (now Brown's Restaurant) designed by John Foster in association with Archibald Ponton and, in the twentieth century, the University of Bristol Dental Hospital and Veterinary School buildings. However, William Paty's death in 1800 is taken here as the end of an era and the end of this study.

The link between the Patys and Bristol was broken at a moment of change for the newly emergent profession of architecture. Neo-classicism was advancing apace and the Gothic Style was evolving from the playful to the deadly serious. William had been experimenting in both styles but it is hard to imagine his operating free from trade. The building industry and architecture were to go their separate ways. He will have known this; after all, he had received, in part at least, a polite education as an 'artistic' designer of buildings at the Royal Academy of Arts but the Patys were linked solidly with the craft of building, through the workshop. William's son, George William might have made the break but he chose a more certain way to middle-class professionalism by taking a commission in one of His Majesty's Regiments of the Line where, when last heard of, he had reached the rank of captain.

The first Paty or Patty recorded in twentieth-century books was a James who became a burgess on the payment of a fine and described by Walter Ison as being registered on March 9th, 1708. In fact he was a 'slip of the pen' and was actually the one I have labelled as James(3) who was declared a burgess 60 years later than this, on March 9th, 1768. His address was 32 Broadmead and it was he who was a carver and gilder who survived – probably as the last of all the Patys with connections in the building trades – until 1807.

The first correctly recorded member of the family is therefore the James who became a burgess on the payment of a fine on April 15th, 1721. A monument by this James dated 1715 in the parish church at Evercreech in Somerset may indicate the family's place of origin. Actually, a conveyance dated December 15th, 1652 between 'William Hobson senior and junior, exec's of the will of Wm Colston and Jas. Patey of Somerton; two messuages in High Street near the High Cross' held in the City Record Office (08022(5)) provides the first known mention of the Patys and confirms their Somerset origins. Perhaps this James was father or grandfather of James (1), whose address was in Merchant Street. He was not apprenticed in Bristol, hence the fine. He died in 1748 and his will does not mention any children. He is credited with the popular Christ Church quarter-jacks and he was the mason/builder of the Old City Library in King Street.

James made a number of very fine wall monuments that show him to have been an excellent stone carver: one at Redcliffe to the Reverend Richard Sandford who died in 1721, and one in Frome Parish Church to Mr. George Locke, who died in 1735, attest to this.

The few contemporary records describe him as 'stone carver' or as a mason but there can be little doubt that he was master mason or architect of the King Street Library and at least one house in College Green was sufficiently similar to it for it to be attributed firmly to him.

This first James did in fact have a son. His will, written in his own hand, was proved only two months after it was written and his wife Rachel must have been pregnant at the time of his death. The son, named after his father, was admitted a free burgess, as already stated, on March 9th, 1768 when he was registered as a carver. His name was entered in the City Apprentice Book for February 23rd, 1760 bound to Thomas Kilby, mason and recorded as 'son of James Patty late of the City of Bristol, carver, deceased'. A lease dated August 17th, 1786 between James Patty, Carver and the Corporation for 'a small messuage in Well Court near Castle Green' described him as 'being about 38 years old' which suggests a birth date in 1748. His father died in February of that year. The will read:

> In the name of God, Amen. This is the last will and testament of me James Patty of Merchant Street, Bristol, carver. First I will and desire that my just debts be satisfied by my executrix hereafter named.
> Also as to all and singular my goods and chattels and personall estate whatsoever – being – I give and bequeath the same unto my dearly beloved wife Rachel Patty, her heirs, administrators, assignees for ever and I do hereby nominate appoint my said dear wife sole executrix of this my last will and hereby revoking all other wills being heretofore made. In witness whereof I have hereunto set my hand and seal this December 21st, 1747
> Witnesses. John Harper. Blacksmith (Old King St.) Ja. Patty
> –ford Morgan.
> Will proved. February 25th, 1747 [Julian Calendar. The year ran from Lady Day, March 25th to March 24th ensuing. The Gregorian Calendar, introduced in 1752 not only started the year on January 1st but it 'stole' eleven days so that February 25th, 1747 would have been March 8th, 1748]

Chronologically, James(1)'s son must be recorded as James(3) because another intervenes who was also recorded as a carver.

James(2) was admitted to 'the Liberties of this City for that he married Mary, daughter of Peter Tonkin, mariner, deceased' in 1755. His address was 21, Horse Street now Host Street, 'Under the Bank'. He died on February 1st, 1779. He was Thomas Paty's younger brother and was his partner. They worked together on the major city development schemes and the first phases of the Clifton layout, although they also worked independently and their workshops always remained separate.

James(2) and Thomas were not the sons of James(1) as Walter Ison suggested in *The Georgian Buildings of Bristol*. They must have been the sons of an unrecorded brother or cousin of his, probably of or from Somerton. James(1) was a burgess of Bristol but they were not the sons of a burgess. James(2) claimed his right through marriage to a burgess's daughter and Thomas, most unusually, never became a freeman at all.

There is no actual record of any formal partnership between the brothers and they certainly worked independently from their separate addresses, but I refer later to the way that Thomas used both his brother and his uncle/aunt/nephew in a federation of workshops in order to gain control of the Bristol building industry. All this happened in a manner that allowed the individual members of the family to operate separately. After James(2)'s death his son John (one of three Johns) announced the continuation of the business in *Felix Farley's Journal* for February and March 1779 where he stated that he 'intended to carry on the business at the Yard Under the Bank in all its branches – monuments, chimney pieces etc. N.B. Land surveying and plans accurately drawn, also measuring.' He had become a free burgess on December 7th, 1778 and was recorded as a carver.

Ten years later at Thomas's death in 1789 his sons made a similar but rather grander announcement in *Bonner and Middleton's Bristol Journal* for May 23rd:

> John and William Paty, architects and statuaries, offer their best thanks to the public for the many favours conferred on them during a partnership with their deceased father which subsisted twelve years. They flatter themselves that unremitting attention, blended with the most scrupulous integrity, will secure a continuance of that patronage they are truly solicitous to merit.

The advertisement was run several times in this and in *Felix Farley's Journal*. They also asked for outstanding bills to be sent in. A week after the last appearance a tragic news item appeared on June 13th, 1789:

> On Wednesday last died at Bath, Mr. John Paty, architect and statuary of this City, a young man of distinguished genius, incorruptable integrity and the most unaffected manners.

So, William was left on his own, to become the only successor to his father's business in Limekiln Lane, below Brandon Hill.

John had become a burgess only weeks before his death. The Burgess Book record for April 22nd, 1789 showed that 'John Paty, architect, is admitted to the liberties of this City for that he married Elizabeth, the daughter of William Perry, mariner deceased and hath taken the oath of obedience and paid £0.4.6d.' He was the second John to be so recorded. He made his will as he lay dying:

> Bath. June 7th, 1789, John Paty, Statuary being weak in body but of sound understanding in this my last will and testament appoint my

> brother William Paty, architect, sole executor. I leave all my effects for my dearly beloved wife Elizabeth and my child, Elizabeth.

Days, or perhaps hours, before his death, he got the professional relationships right; he was the one trained as a sculptor whilst his brother was the architect. In fact, John was also to sire a son, born posthumously, just as his uncle had done 41 years previously. This information was recorded in his brother's will, proven in 1801 where William left a legacy 'to my nephew John son of my late brother John'.

John's will and his father's were proved together on August 3rd, 1789 before the Reverend John Complin. Thomas had died on May 4th, 1789 whilst John died on or a day or so after June 7th. Thomas's will showed him to have been well-to-do if not wealthy:

> Dated May 2nd, 1789.
> I hereby give and bequeath to my daughter Elizabeth King wife of Thomas King statuary, of the City of Bath, the sum of eight hundred pounds to be paid by my executors and I further will and declare that the said sum after the decease of the said Elizabeth King be settled on her son, Charles King provided she has no other issue but in case of other children by the said Thomas King, to be equally divided between them but should Elizabeth King die without issue it is my will that she has the sole disposal of the said money.
> I also give and bequeath the aforementioned Thomas King the sum of £250 for his sole use benefit and disposal.
> I further give and bequeath to my son John Paty such a sum of money as shall be judged adequate to the then value of a dwelling house in Park Street in the City of Bristol given to and settled on Sarah Hickes at her marriage with my son William Paty. The said house to be valued by such referees as the said John and William Paty shall appoint and their determination to be binding to both parties in respect to such money to be paid or accounted for by the said William Paty. This my will and testament being fulfilled I do appoint my sons John and William Paty, Joint executors of all my effects both real and personal after paying my just debts in testemony whereof I sign this in the presence of my children.
> Jno Paty. William Paty. Eliz. King. Thos. Paty.

On the back of this a note read 'August 3rd, 1789. Proved. Oath of William Paty', and noted that John Paty had died before this.

It is extraordinary that Thomas Paty made no reference to John Paty's wife and child whilst he made detailed provision for his daughter's husband and child and William's wife, Sarah. His separate legacy to John was a means of equalising the residue of the estate between the brothers by accounting for the marriage settlement of the house in Park Street. Why was no settlement made for John and Elizabeth at the time of their marriage? No other Paty document prompts one to ask personal questions about relationships. Had John and William kept the marriage from the old man? Had the old man disapproved of Elizabeth? This document begins to lift a veil but it doesn't lift it far. Only the most tentative questions can be asked, but there is a hint of drama. With so little information about the Paty dynasty, any scrap of information may be used to lead one forward or even backwards. Was John's untimely death a real burden for William, or was it, secretly, a relief? We shall never know, though William did describe the loss as 'a catastrophy' and one can assume that there was a strong bond between them. After all, he left a legacy for John's posthumous son in his will.

William's marriage to Sarah Hickes, the daughter of the late Alderman Hickes which took place in January, 1784, did not allow him free access to the Burgess List. He was enrolled on December 9th, 1790 on the payment of a fine of 15 guineas required of those who were not the sons of Freemen, or apprenticed in the City or married to the daughter of a Freeman. The Alderman was a 'foreigner' from the County of Gloucestershire.

Bristol directories began to appear in the 1770s. The first was *Sketchley's Directory* of 1775 which recorded four Paty addresses. There was James(2) at 21 Horse Street, William in 6 Lamb Street (only seventeen and away from home), James(3) (successor to James(1)) in 32 Broadmead and Thomas with his eldest son in Limekiln Lane. At the end of the decade, three names survived in the lists. They were William Paty, Architect and Statuary, Successor to Thomas Paty and Sons, of Limekiln Lane and College Place, John Paty(1) successor to James Paty(2), Carver and Mason, Horse Street (under the bank), James Paty(3) (successor to James Paty(1)) carver and gilder of Merchant Street. By 1791 only William and James(3) remained in the directory.

John(1) does not seem to have survived in Horse Street. His entry disappears from the directories but he was recorded as having voted for the Whig politician Cruger in the January 1781 election and was then living in St. Augustine's parish. It may be that by then he was working for his uncle Thomas and living in or near Limekiln Lane.

James Paty(3), born in 1748, after his father's death, actually achieved a slightly longer than average lifespan for a Paty. *Felix Farley's Journal* recorded that he died 'On Saturday August 29th, 1807 in his sixtieth year'. He was described as 'Mr Patty, Carver and Gilder'. Only Thomas lived longer.

There is no proven link between the Broadmead Patys (more often called Patty) and the other two branches in Limekiln Lane and Horse Street, but there is circumstantial evidence that makes the link between James(1) and Thomas and his brother James more or less certain. First, there is the established fact that Thomas, as a young man, called on James(1) to help him out in carving the capitals for the giant order of Corinthian pilasters for the Exchange, when he had difficulty in meeting a deadline there.

James(1) was then a senior figure amongst the Bristol masons, so it is possible that Thomas turned to his well known and reliable namesake rather than his uncle, for help, but the other circumstance is more nearly certain. This involves the so-called Paty Copybook which contains designs that match monuments in churches that were made by Patys from Limekiln Lane, Horse Street and from Merchant Street.

It is demonstrable that monuments signed by James Paty and made between 1720 and 1748 must have been made by James(1), whilst those made between 1755 when James(2) became a Freeman, and 1768 when James(3) came out of his articles, must have been by James(2). Between 1768 and 1775 when James(2) died, they could be by either, and after 1775, James Paty monuments can only be by James(3).

Thus, drawing No. 92 in the copybook, identified with a monument in Evercreech Church, dated 1715 is by James(1). Drawing No.37 is identified as a drawing for a monument in St. Thomas Church dated 1735 and therefore by James(1). The monument stands beside another which is very similar to the neighbouring drawing, No.38 but it is dated 1767 and so must be by James Paty(2). This poses a difficulty because the two drawings are apparently by the same hand. No.38 appears at All Saints twice and at Henbury Parish Church too. All are dated in the 1760s and, as James(1) and(2) were only cousins and operated independently it may be that an alternative scenario with James(1)'s 'dearly beloved wife, Rachel' continuing the business after her husband's death until her son grew up to take on the burden.

Whatever the reality, I am certain that Drawing No.s 37, 38 and 39 were by the same hand and that hand was James Paty(1)'s. Drawings 89 and 93 are for monuments carrying profile portraits and these seem to be the province of James(2). John Foy's monument in St. James Church, dated 1771, is one of these and there are others in All Saints and St Thomas's.

Other drawings in the Copybook by James Paty(1) on stylistic and draughtsmanship evidence are No.s 28 and 122. Two designs seem to be late in date, are by an excellent draughtsman, much better than Henry Wood, and are sophisticated beyond Mr. Wood's capacities and I suggest that they are by James Paty(3). These are No.s 115 and 123.

The Copybook is not in its original binding or order but there is no doubt that drawings of monuments made by James Paty(1) and (2) and probably (3) exist there, with Thomas and William and John's as well as some by Henry Wood, and this firmly establishes a link between the Broadmead and the Horse Street Patys and thereby with the Limekiln Lane ones, too.

The Paty dynasty comprised two branches, operating out of three addresses. The first worked from 32 Broadmead and later from Merchant Street, namely

James(1) and his posthumous son James(3). The second, working from Limekiln Lane and Horse Street, were Thomas and his brother James(2) and their children, John, William and John.

To summarise, the members of the family who were significant to Bristol's building history were:

James Pat(t)y(1), born before 1700, whose first traced work is dated 1715, was elected a burgess on payment of a fine in 1721. This address was Broadmead and later, Merchant Street, Broadmead and he died in 1748.

James Paty(2), brother of Thomas Paty, became a free burgess in 1755 on marriage to a burgess's daughter, and lived in 21 Horse Street (Under the Bank) and who died in 1779.

Thomas Paty, born 1713, never became a burgess, lived in Limekiln Lane and died in 1789.

James Paty(3), son of James(1), was born, 1748, became a free burgess in 1768, lived in Merchant Street and died in 1807.

John Paty(1) was born in the 1750s, son of James(2). Became free burgess in 1778, lived in 21 Horse Street, died perhaps before Thomas Paty.

John Paty(2), eldest son of Thomas Paty, was born 1754 and became a free burgess on marriage to a burgess's daughter in 1789 and died the same year, lived in Limekiln Lane.

William Paty, younger son of Thomas Paty, born 1757, became burgess on payment of a fine in 1790. Lived in Limekiln Lane and College Place. Died 1800.

John Paty(3), posthumous son of John Paty(2), was born 1789/90.

George William Paty, Son of William Paty, date of birth not known but was a Captain in the 32nd Regiment of Foot and had reached 21 years in 1809.

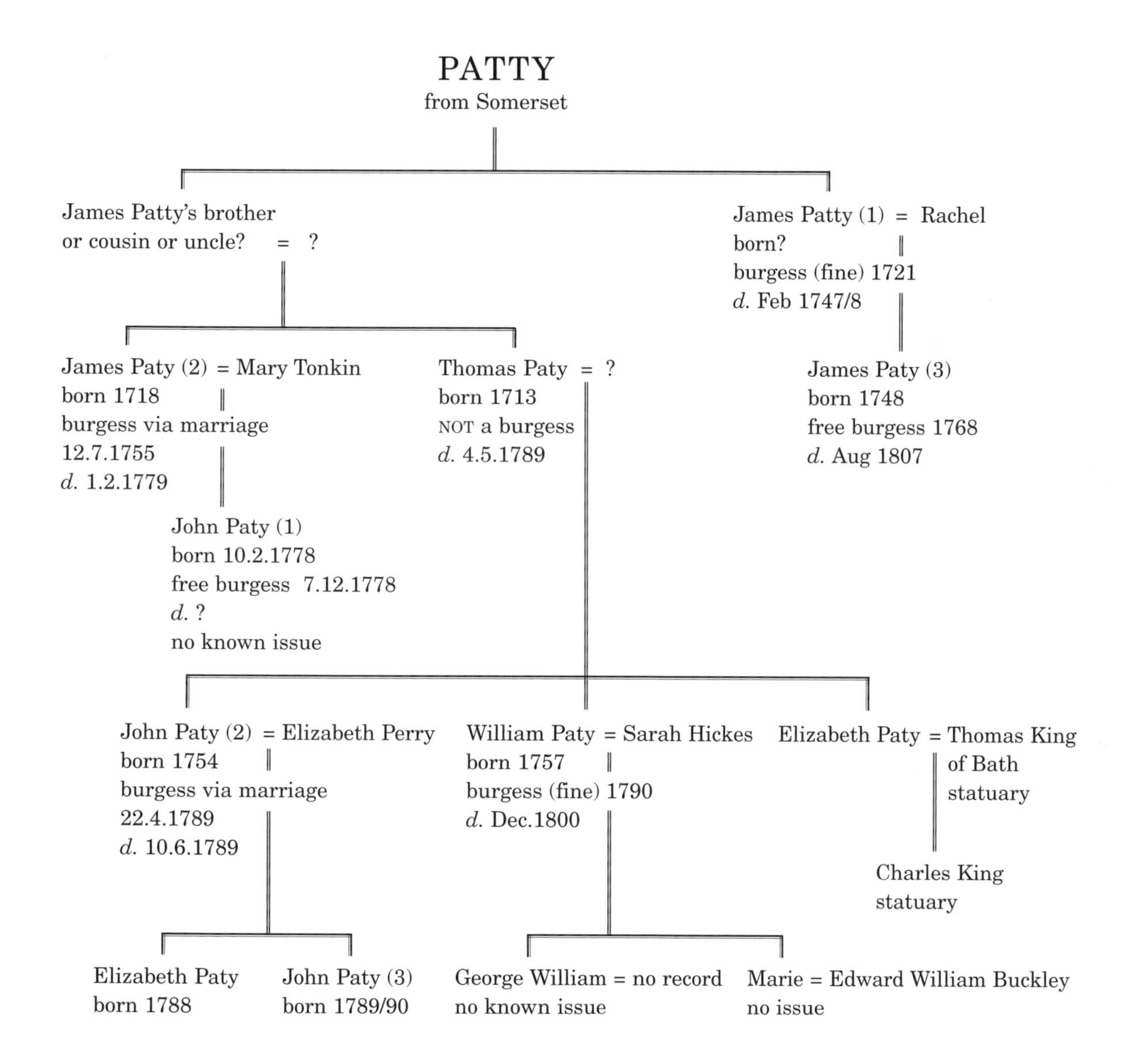
PATTY
from Somerset
James Patty's brother
or cousin or uncle? = ?
James Patty (1) = Rachel
born?
burgess (fine) 1721
d. Feb 1747/8
James Paty (2) = Mary Tonkin
born 1718
burgess via marriage
12.7.1755
d. 1.2.1779
Thomas Paty = ?
born 1713
NOT a burgess
d. 4.5.1789
James Paty (3)
born 1748
free burgess 1768
d. Aug 1807
John Paty (1)
born 10.2.1778
free burgess 7.12.1778
d. ?
no known issue
John Paty (2) = Elizabeth Perry
born 1754
burgess via marriage
22.4.1789
d. 10.6.1789
William Paty = Sarah Hickes
born 1757
burgess (fine) 1790
d. Dec.1800
Elizabeth Paty = Thomas King
of Bath
statuary
Charles King
statuary
Elizabeth Paty
born 1788
John Paty (3)
born 1789/90
George William = no record
no known issue
Marie = Edward William Buckley
no issue

James Paty(1)

The first eighteenth-century reference to a Paty in the City Record Office is to the James who was made a burgess in 1721, who was stone mason and carver on the new Library in King Street in 1739–41 and who carved and painted the quarter-jacks on the Christ Church (City) tower. He usually signed himself with two Ts and his address was 21 Merchant Street, Broadmead where his workshop was. He worked in stone and wood, was called carver and gilder, and never considered himself to be anything other than a tradesman. The carvings on the King Street Library and most of the architectural details have been destroyed or defaced and the quarter-jacks, in painted wood, belong to a folk tradition rather than a sculptural one, but a number of mural monuments in churches demonstrate his worth as an artist.

The first of these is dated 1715, several years before his entry onto the Bristol Burgess list, and is in Evercreech Parish Church. It is dedicated to the memory of Mr Joseph Barker and the design matches part of an important drawing (92) in the Paty Copybook. This is larger than average, more free and bold in execution than most of the other drawings, and stands out as being by someone other than Thomas or William, the most usual contributors. It shows a plain rectangular wall panel on a yellow marble backing with narrow consol brackets at each side and an elaborate 'marmalade' marble base with a curved, stepped and reverse curved lower edge. A winged cherub's head is mounted on this. The base has a narrow plain edge strip and is flanked by a pair of rectangular blocks, carrying medallions and with foliate supporters. Above, a cornice and plain strip provides the base for a short curved sided 'pyramid' of white marble that forms the background for the bust of a man. He wears a toga and is surrounded by military trophies. Above this, a second cornice topped by a pair of 'recumbent' consols, which in their turn support a wreath and a heraldic badge, but the badge is left blank.

Mr Barker's monument at Evercreech lacks the pyramid with its sculptured bust and the trophies but is otherwise very similar. The drawing is by James Paty(1) and must date from the time of the monument, making it the earliest drawing in the book.

Two better known monuments by James(1) are that to the Rev. Richard Sandford in St. Mary Redcliffe, dated 1721 and inscribed 'Ia Paty fecit', and that to George Locke in Frome Parish Church, dated 1735 and signed 'I (or J) Paty, Bristol fecit'. Although they are a long way apart in date they are very similar. Mr Locke's is larger and in some ways grander, being over three

Copybook drawing No.92, by James Paty(1)

Monument in Frome Parish Church to George Locke, 1735

Detail from the George Locke monument

Monument in St Mary Redcliffe Church, Bristol to the Reverend Richard Sandford, 1721

metres high and having a more complex base with a cherub's head and a splendid scatter of roses in a swag between the baroque consols that support the columns flanking the monument. The columns are of the composite order in both. These beautiful memorials are outstanding examples of early to mid-century carving and suggest that James(1) was a designer and sculptor of importance who perhaps outshone his younger relatives and descendants.

Unfortunately, some of the buildings James is thought to have been involved with have not been well treated or have not survived. The one to which a claim for design authorship is strongest, the Old Library in King Street, was comprehensively mutilated by Bristol's City Architect in or before 1951. A superb but crumbling civic coat of arms was chiselled off the pediment in order to avoid the cost of repair. Similar treatment eliminated two charming carved panels over the first floor windows that depicted 'putti studying books, the arts and sciences'. At the same time, all the mouldings on the cornice, the pediment, over the windows and elsewhere were cut back to the root. The front door survives although the modelling of the dentilled cornice and pediment have been mutilated as elsewhere. Incidentally, the use of the composite order, then unusual in Bristol except by James(1), suggests that he was not merely sculptor and mason, but was in charge of the design as a whole. It is difficult now to appreciate the building as it was before it was so brutally treated, but it is just possible to note that it was once a structure of good proportion and sensitivity, unusual in eighteenth-century Bristol before the building of John Wood's Exchange. In his book, *The Eighteenth Century Architecture of Bristol* published in 1923, C.F.W. Dening reported that the 'building was rapidly falling into decay' so we are lucky that it is still standing. Perhaps the mouldings, at least, could be replaced one day.

A house in College Green that bore a distinct resemblance to the King Street Library was destroyed during the war, in 1940/1. This was No. 32 and was built in the early 1740s. It was of five bays with the central three set forward and pedimented. It had a dentilled cornice and a carved tympanum and was in proportion and detail very similar to King Street, although the tall first floor of the library was replaced by the two upper floors of the town mansion that this was. The front door no longer existed in the 1940s when it was destroyed; it had then long since been altered into a shop, and was the grand J.F. Taylor and Sons: 'Taylors of the Green'. No early photographs seem to exist which would show whether James's composite column front door was there. As well as the general disposition of elements suggesting the same designer for both, there was also the use of carved panels, this time of knotted and tasseled swags under, rather than over, two of the upper floor windows.

The only other Bristol building of the 1730s to 40s that used the free floating carved-panel motif used at King Street and College Green is at Redland Court where three carvings appear above the central first-floor windows, under the pediment. Here, the swags are garlanded and on the centre one a pair of quivers give additional enrichment. Redland Court is firmly established as by John Strahan but the quality of the carving on the front and on the splendid gate piers, below, very strongly suggests James Paty as sculptor.

Above the central windows, there is a detail that appears to be struggling towards the detail used on the Exchange a few years later, where John Wood, with the young Thomas Paty in tow, burst into the final decorative formula that Andrea Palladio used in his unfinished Casa del Diavolo at Vicenza with the spaces between the Corinthian capitals carved so that the whole zone, and not just the capitals, was decorated. The use of Ionic order here prevented this in any case, but there is a clear suggestion of the free-floating swags moving upwards to make a final Palladian statement.

To return to the centre of the city, it seems that James Paty(1)'s last decade was a busy one if he was involved in all the buildings that have been associated with his name. Walter Ison suggested that he was concerned with several houses in College Green and that he built the terrace of three houses in Unity Street as well. If that was the case, they stand as a physical and symbolic start to the Paty family's advance into Clifton.

No. 30 College Green is the only grand house remaining in the area and nothing is left of its original character externally. It was a house of some grandeur, however, with a giant Ionic order of pilasters at the middle three bays of a five-bay structure and with a fine pulvinated and modillioned cornice. It is possible that originally the whole front was of brick with Bath stone dressings or it may even be that the whole front was a plaster sham. This would explain why the Ionic capitals and the gigantic keystones and cornices over the first-floor windows disappeared when the house was repaired after war damage. If this had been the case, it was more than an unusual house that should have been properly restored, it was a unique building in this area, and should not have been subjected to the restoration of the late 1980s when it was rerendered and treated to an overall application of plastic or timber 'keystones' that turned it into an anonymous late 1980s neo-Georgian office block. The photograph in the Dening book would allow the accurate restoration that should now be undertaken. In its way the deplorable, unthinking recent 'restoration' is less forgivable than the cost-saving mishandling of the Old Library in 1950.

Whether or not this was a James Paty(1) design remains uncertain, but the house was probably originally intended to be in stone. The bases for the giant pilasters were cut and set in stone and can still be seen above the High-Victorian shop front.

The group of houses comprising the main element of Unity Street was built between 1742 and 1745 and because it was an attempt at a 'palace front' in Bath stone it was perhaps showing the influence of John Wood, whose presence during the building of the Exchange was strongly felt. The three houses on a steep slope are forced into the palace format (almost), with the

The Old City Library, King Street, Bristol, as photographed c.1924

The Old City Library in 2001, after the removal of carved coat of arms, plaque and some moulding

32 College Green (now demolished)

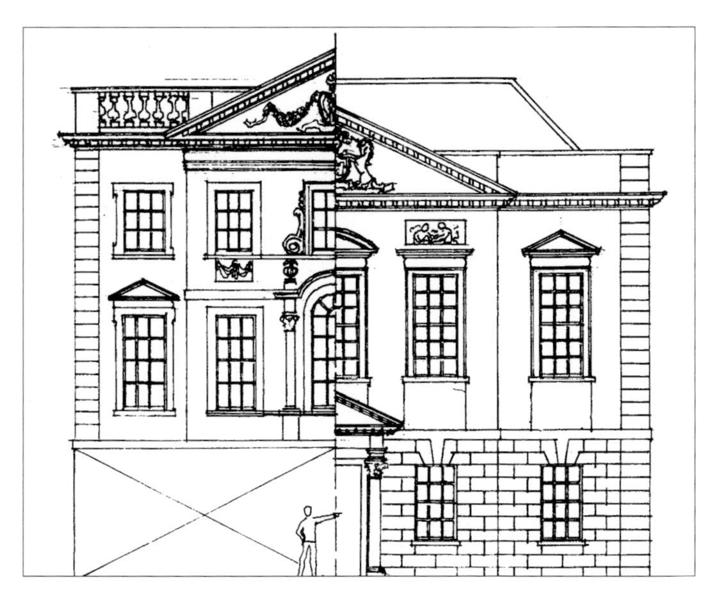

Comparative drawing of the Old City Library (right)
and 32 College Green (left)

30 College Green in 1924 and (below) in 2001

Unity Street in 1924 and (below) in 2001

lowest one built up out of the ground and the upper one taken into the ground to allow the cornice to run continuously on a horizontal plane. The windows and floors should have done so too, but instead a Bristol compromise was reached. The cornice stayed level but the windows stepped up and, in order to demonstrate that it did not matter, the window heads were changed into segments. Actually, of course, it did matter. Otherwise, the terrace is a careful and correct piece of work, which set the stage for the construction of Park Street. Again, there is no evidence of James(1)'s involvement here but other than the basic solecism of the windows, there is care and an honesty about the design that makes him the most likely originator of the street that the Corporation called 'Unity' in loyal celebration of the fact that the Prince of Wales and the King had ceased to quarrel for a while.

In the absence of firm evidence, James Paty(1)'s worth as an architect is very difficult to assess. There are facts about the quality of his carving and the design of the objects that he certainly made. The fact that he called himself a carver and never apparently proposed himself as designer (a word that he probably never knew) has allowed him to be overlooked and perhaps displaced by others. It has been shown that every three-dimensional element of the King Street building was made (and designed) by him. No one has claimed that another person was in charge of the disposition of those elements in space, and it is reasonable to assume that he was responsible for the construction of the interior elements of the Library too: the staircase, the fireplace under the Gibbons overmantel and the vigorous book presses, now all in the Central Library. There cannot be much doubt that he was indeed the architect here. For the other attributions, there is less to go on.

I have drawn the elevations of the King Street Library and No. 32 College Green to scale, by using Mr. Dening's photographs which had measuring rods placed on them. They could well have been by the same hand, but the similarities are not as apparent as I had hoped. What does come out is that the King Street building is, or was before it was mutilated, simple, honest and mature whilst the College Green house was overstated and rather pompous. It could be that these differences of approach demonstrate the differences in the two clients, the one trusting a respected craftsman to provide a dignified and cheap, but efficient, Library, whilst the other demanded a building that expressed wealth and importance from a man who was happier when designing modestly.

At Redland Court, it is clear that John Strahan was architect, but I wonder whether he was the designer. It is distinctly odd that he should have used John Jacob de Wilstar, one of the City Surveyors, to draw up the presentation design for his client; de Wilstar was at best only semi-literate architecturally. Some of his other drawings are in the Bristol Record Office and have been described by Walter Ison as having 'the engaging naïvety of some early cartography'. He could perhaps have produced the bizarre designs for the Kingsmead Square, Bath, and Queen Charlotte Street houses, but not this rather sophisticated design. It could be that James Paty(1) and he collaborated on this important project.

John Strahan could well have been less than good as a designer and he might indeed have leaned on others for this skill. There is no reason to assume that only present-day architects sometimes borrow others' skill to reinforce their own. My interest is in James Paty(1), however, and it has to be said that there is no evidence that he ghosted for Mr. Strahan. He saw himself as a skilled craftsman and he worked at Redland Court. At the very least, he was a worthy precursor of the Paty dynasty.

In a later chapter, I suggest that Thomas Paty designed Redland Chapel, but I think that James was involved, too. The Ionic order used on the Chapel and the Court and on 30 College Green make the link. Although they were not identical, they were clearly from the same Gibbsian source. The masterly west elevation and its cupola were produced under Thomas's control, although the Ionic order will have been pre-selected by James, perhaps deferring to his client's desires. It may be that the upset that occurs with the east and west ends at war with each other is a result of James pushing on with the building whilst Thomas was still designing, probably delaying whilst he was under pressure from John Wood and his masons on the Exchange where he was being required to produce Corinthian capitals, the swags between them and the royal coat of arms, at precisely this time. James is recorded as helping by producing two of the Corinthian capitals for his nephew. James was a good man, always ready to oblige, but not an architect. This perhaps is why Mr. Cozens was later to ask Mr. Halfpenny to take over the works here.

I finish this discussion of James Paty(1) by looking at Earnshill. There is documentary evidence of this house near Curry Rivel in Somerset being completed in 1731, which upsets my previously held theory that the drawings were by Thomas Paty as they were found in the same portfolio as his drawings for Ston Easton House. Although the draughtsmanship is not the same as the other drawings, there is a similarity to drawings number 28 and 92 in the Paty Copybook, both by James Paty(1).

I am now satisfied that the drawings are by James as preliminary drawings for Earnshill, made either in his own right or on behalf of another. (John Strahan's name was associated with Earnshill by Christopher Hussey in his *Country Life* articles on the house in 1960.)

The drawings consist of two elevations and some plans of a large house of two main floors on a basement. They show what appears to be a rendered front with stone string courses and architraved windows with a triangular modillioned pediment over the central three bays of a seven-bayed house with modillioned cornice and blank parapets elsewhere.

Earnshill itself is faced in brick above a stone basement, and has five bays, flanked by two bay connectors which link to extensive wings enclosing a deep courtyard on the south. A comparison between the drawings and the actual house reveal many differences; the house is of five bays at the centre, it has a stone rustic basement, stone quoins and a stone frieze. The two front doors are also different as are the staircases to them in layout. Almost everything is different and yet the similarity between the drawings and the actuality is strong enough for one to be certain that they were drawings for Earnshill and made by a Paty. Because of the dating and other evidence, this Paty must have been James(1). Unity Street in Bristol makes a good comparison. It must have been built after Earnshill but there are strong similarities in feeling.

The house has a strong baroque character, as one would expect in provincial England in the 1720s and 1730s. The deep narrow courtyard with its ground floor blind arcade (masked now by planting) is the strongest feature, leading up to the entrance; also almost Vanbrugh-like are the storey-high brackets that mark the change of level between the central block and the wings. Internally, although there is a Bristol feel of quiet simplicity, the spatial organisation with the two identical staircases opening onto a vast space on each of three floors is a baroque feature.

The pair of staircases is the most unusual feature. In some respects they are quite typical Bristol staircases in oak. They have a magnificent 'going' so they would be marvellous for promenading richly dressed notables, as are the spaces onto which they open. Yet in all details but one they are handsome but ordinary. The ends of stairs are finished with beautifully carved brackets and the soffits are modelled in wood to the shape of the brackets just as they are in several Bristol houses. There is just one change from the standard: in the balusters, where instead of the usual three there are just two massive Tuscan columns alternately plain and twisted, on each step supporting a very bulky but handsome handrail. This detail seems somehow to lift the whole into a bigger scale.

The exotic saloon fireplace I first took to have been imported direct from Italy but I now think it sprang direct from James Paty's imagination and his workshop. It is both vast and full of rare Italian marbles used in profusion, and astonishingly it has at its centre a gigantic classical pot, so beloved of monumental masons. All the other fireplaces in the house seem to be of a later period, mostly from the 1760s and doubtless were a result of change in ownership. It is, of course, still possible that the house lay incomplete and unlived in until the Combes family took over in 1758 but the stairs and probably the saloon fireplace must date from the earlier period.

Henry Combe was a Bristol merchant and mayor of the city. He was very much aware of the Paty family, and purchasing an existing Paty house might well have been next best to commissioning one. The house seems to express exactly what the ambitious Combes desired, yet the evidence is clear that it

Earnshill, Somerset

was built by another family, the Eyles of Devizes, who had advanced further than the Combes, for they had sent two of their family to Westminster as MPs, but had fallen through involvement with the notorious South Sea Bubble scandal. They had lost their fortune ten years before they started on the building of Earnshill. Perhaps their dreams for their house were similar to those of their successors who were in search of power through Royal patronage. Henry Combe's son Richard was the owner of a diamond-studded snuffbox which had been presented to him by Frederick, Prince of Wales, in 1738, when he was just 12 years old. It remained a symbol of his dream of patronage, for which Earnshill seemed a possible means.

Earnshill, then, was designed by James Paty(1), and designed as a backdrop to grand ceremony. Whether James stood on his own feet or as an agent of Strahan's we may never know, but the quality of the masonry and particularly of the brick-work suggests that a Bristol master was on site, just as James(1) was at Redland Court, a year or so later.

James Paty (2)

James Paty(2) was a younger brother of the better known Thomas; but he died in 1779, ten years before his brother. His workshop was in 21 Horse (now Host) Street and his career was independent, although he was in partnership with Thomas in some of the entrepreneurial ventures of street improvements and new layouts in the city, in Park Street and in Clifton.

He had been credited in the past with the design of the Theatre Royal but the design and construction were in fact carried out by Thomas and the only major building that James is known to have been involved in is Stoke Park although it seems that the design was another's.

A number of monuments in the city and elsewhere signed Jas Paty can be ascribed to him with some, though not absolute, certainty because of their dates between 1747 when James(1) died and 1768 when James(3) completed his apprenticeship. The exceptions are discussed in the chapter on the Paty Copybook. It seems that Rachel Paty kept her late husband's workshop ticking over between the two dates. As a sculptor and designer, James(2) was competent and individual but not outstanding. He sometimes carved portrait profiles of the deceased, and he tended towards a rather old-fashioned baroque technique in his work. This can be seen in the designs numbered 89 and 93 in the copybook where profile portraits appear on drawings that are distinctly different technically from the usual.

A series of monuments of the right date, signed Jas or James Paty exist in the churches of SS Philip and Jacob, All Saints and St Thomas, that carry portrait heads of the deceased on *bas relief* medallions in distinctly old-fashioned designs. A few monuments like these by James(2) from the 1760s and 70s have been traced to churches in Monmouth and Brecon. Between them they establish a distinctive and rather idiosyncratic style that separates the work quite clearly from that of his brother and sons.

Stoke Park was rebuilt in the 1760s. This is a house that has been forgotten by Bristol historians and is only now 'coming into view' after the National Health Service has given up its long tenancy. Standing on its artificial promontary above the M32 motorway it is well known to Bristolians and visitors as an object of distant drama rather than as a piece of real architecture. At the time of writing in 2003, the house was being converted into luxury flats and a large residential estate was being developed in the grounds behind.

Its character is much affected by a bold, single-storey pavilion that fills the space between the projecting wings of the southerly aspect of the house.

The detailing is strange. The pavilion has five bays of semi-circular-headed windows with bold, square springings that make a strong horizontal emphasis. Each window has a keystone that runs into a string course that links the windows together horizontally and defines the bottom of the parapet, which is mainly solid with vertical shafts to mark the bays, running from the string course to the coping and finished below the string course with a 'dagger' of stone, which echoes the keystone at the window heads. Thus, a rather insistent rhythm is set up which is enhanced by the shafts being projected upwards beyond the coping to make a sort of castellation. This odd detailing is raised to the bizarre by the introduction of another element. Between the bay shafts, over the middle of the windows, the coping is raised to enclose a square of space which forms a more dominant castellation than that provided by the over-riding bay shafts. All of this is shown on an engraved view to have been created by Thomas Wright to fit the Jacobean house, before the Paty intervention.

Beyond the pavilion, the house is solid and plain. Two massive bay windows almost fill the south elevation of the arms that enclose the pavilion. They rise three floors and the roof is hidden by parapets, which, over the central section of the bays, is raised in a gestural piece of 'fortification', in this case entirely unconvincing. The detail is repeated around the corner on the body of the house where they look like, and possibly were, chimney stacks.

It is now suggested that James Paty(2) was site architect and main contractor, under the design control of the enigmatic Thomas Wright, Norborne Berkeley's landscape architect. In fact, the house generally is a rather ordinary, if not run-of-the-mill design, from the outside. Apart from the pavilion, it is unusually plain, entirely lacking the attributes of a house of this importance in the social set-up of mid-eighteenth century England. It is without colonnades, pediments, cornices or rustication. It is mainly rendered with a very modest decoration of stone dressings.

Eileen Harris shows, in her introductory essay to the facsimile edition of Wright's *Arbors and Grottos* that Wright was in fact the designer, intent on making the house subservient to the planting plan. This strange 'poly-mathematical genius' who was said to be 'utterly devoid of an ability to manage his practical affairs and to make capital of his gifts …' was the first scientist in the world to suggest that the 'Milky Way' was in fact millions of stars and not just a local cloud of dust, and who had been tutor in Mathematics and Astronomy to Frederick, Prince of Wales until the prince's untimely death in 1751.

Wright became more interested in his second profession of landscape design after that time, perhaps sometimes improving on and certainly paralleling his contemporary, Launcelot Brown in the development of the Romantic Landscape Garden. His interest in architecture was probably less strong and he thought of himself as an amateur like some of his aristocratic clients.

The appointment of James Paty(2) and/or Thomas Paty to cope with the 'grimy reality' of the building works at Stoke Park, probably demonstrates Wright's limitations. The job was actually, at least in part, the reconstruction of a pre-existing Jacobean mansion and the practical skills of a Paty would have been much needed. It is no longer possible to decide how much of the building was Paty-inspired, but as Thomas Wright was intent on allowing the building to merge with the planting he could well have restrained his executant from extravagant expenditure! It is probable that the extraordinary pavilion with its strange detailing is, directly, Thomas Wright-inspired, as is the form of the house as a whole, which is as romantic an idea as anything by Sir John Vanbrugh. It has a very strong 'castle air', sitting on its Jacobean terrace, and, were it not for the new housing, one could imagine it, with judicious planting, being turned into an instant ruin. It seems that Thomas Wright's intention was to create a building with a vaguely medieval air by constructing corner towers and crenellating the whole thing. In the event, the James Paty-bay windows stood in for the fortress towers and the castellations just did not happen, except for the very uncertain repeat of the pavilion's roof detail in one or two places.

Internally, nothing very notable happens. Both Thomas Paty and his plasterer Thomas Stocking were paid for work completed there, but James was in charge and his solid, no nonsense common sense won through. The whole house was completed with an orderly ordinariness that seems to have been James' hallmark; yet, in its dramatic setting, it comes through as an important romantic statement of Thomas Wright's.

Thomas Paty

Thomas Paty was in his seventy-seventh year when he died on May 4th, 1789, which confirms that he was born in 1712 or 1713 rather than 1718 as Walter Ison suggested. His father was not James Paty(1) but an as yet unidentified brother or cousin of his. There is no evidence to suggest that Thomas was born in Bristol, but by 1739 at the age of 26 when he began employment for the Corporation under John Wood, as stone carver on the Exchange, he was well known to the Civic Committee for the Building and was treated as a favoured native son.

In the course of a long professional life, he worked in partnership with his brother James(2) on a number of the City Development (new streets) projects between 1755 and 1779 when James died. Their workshops remained quite separate during all this time. From 1776 onwards, he worked in association with his sons John(2) and William who had returned to Bristol from London, where they had been students at the Royal Academy, John in sculpture from 1772 and William in architecture in 1775. After their induction, the firm was known as Thomas Paty and Sons.

The young Thomas Paty had made his name, as far as the aldermen were concerned, by the time of his employment at the Exchange. His commission to do the Hilliard monument in the Lord Mayor's Chapel came after this. This was perhaps the biggest memorial of the eighteenth century raised in a Bristol church. It is in several parts. It starts at ground level with a plain, architectural semicircular headed opening into the vault in Bath stone, rusticated with a bold keystone and voussoirs, contained at top and bottom with plain base and string course or capping band, which provides the sub-base for three separate plinths on their own bases. The two outer ones form short columns of white-veined marble which support a pair of fully three-dimensional mourning *putti*. Both carry loose and inadequate cloaks, draped over their marvellously rendered locks and some parts of their anatomies. One holds an end of his stone cloth to wipe away a tear. They lean, disconsolate against a funerary casket, the centre point of the monument, borne up on the middle plinth. It carries carved details of Mr. Hilliard's life and benefactions. Above the casket is a carved portrait bust. If this is by Thomas Paty, and there is no reason to doubt it, he deserves a place amongst the most important English sculptors of that time. It is a brilliant piece of work. It depicts a rather solemn person wearing an informal, loose fitting cap. A cloak covers his right shoulder and outlines his left. He wears a high-collared jacket, buttoned to the neck. The bust stands on a dark plinth and is supported by a pair of 'recumbent' consol brackets in

Monument to William Hilliard by Thomas Paty in the
Lord Mayor's Chapel, College Green

white marble. The dark plinth matches the funeral casket, which has a waist of heavy gadrooning topped with an ovolo and a semi-circular bead. Below the gadrooning, the casket is a truncated conoid and it bears a white marble plaque recording the fact that Mr. Hilliard was born in Seahouse in the parish of Ilminster in Somerset.

The background to the bust is a white marble slab which is capped with a broken pediment and cornice supported by a pair of consol brackets. A frieze below the broken pediment appears just at the brackets so that it reads as two square blocks, almost like metopes, supporting the ears of the broken pediment. Within the tympanum, immediately above Mr. Hilliard's head, is a carved, draped curtain, held open around the head.

All this might seem to be sufficient to record the life of this otherwise quite forgotten justice of the peace but the monument continues upwards as a marble obelisk which rises almost to the ceiling of the chapel, filling its corner of the south aisle. The obelisk is stopped with a flambeau, and, in the centre of the pyramid is Mr. Hilliard's heraldic device, surrounded by a laurel wreath. It is a deeply impressive monument in praise of a man whose name now means nothing beyond the glory of the stones. It is certainly the finest of all eighteenth-century memorials in Bristol and establishes Thomas Paty's reputation as a designer and sculptor.

There is no drawing in the copybook that can be taken as a prototype for this design although several are comparable to parts of it, particularly No. 87 with its mourning cherub. It is clear from the evidence of the copybook and from extant monuments in the City and elsewhere that Thomas was a brilliant sculptor and was the most successful of the Bristol monumental masons of that time, but his main contribution was to be as a developer-architect.

In architecture, his career started as a subsidiary contributor on a number of important projects. He worked under John Wood the Elder at the Exchange where he provided all the main architectural embellishments including the three splendid coats of arms. The Royal Coat on the north front to Corn Street is the crowning element in a brilliant composition as was the Bristol Coat on the south, designed to be seen from the Place of Exchange but now only visible from the first floor rooms above the glazed roof of the Exchange, and finally, the Bristol badge over the Market Square elevation which has the unicorns replaced by a flourish of acanthus leaves. The Exchange is Bristol's most important eighteenth-century building; it is regarded as John Wood the Elder's monument but it is also Thomas Paty's monument.

Thomas was involved with the stone and timber carving at Redland Chapel where he was at work before the Exchange got under way. Indeed, it could well be that John Wood saw his work there, approved and decided to use him at the Exchange. There is still a question about the designer of this building. The two most recent books suggest and assert respectively that John Strahan was the architect although he died probably well before the beginning of the contract.

John Wood the Elder's Exchange, Corn Street, Bristol: royal coat of arms and embellishments by Thomas Paty
[photo: John Trelawny-Ross]

This subject has long exercised the minds of architectural historians. The only documentary evidence available is that William Halfpenny signed a contract on May 22nd, 1742 in which he agreed

> with John Cousins Esqr to give proper directions as is usual by architects and Directors of Buildings, to All his workmen employ'd at his Chapple at Redland, and to see said Workmen do their Work in a Workmanlike Manner and see that they make proper use of his Materials without Waste, and to see the whole completed for the sum of Ten Pounds Ten shillings sterling.
> I said Halfpenny do Agree to visit said Work six days in evry Week and for Evry Day Neglect, I do agree to Forfit Three Shillings And Sixpence and to Measure all Said Work when required, both within and without.
> William Halfpenny.

According to Walter Ison, all the external stone carving, the exquisite lime-wood recently dreadfully damaged by vandals, all the cherubs and the architectural plasterwork inside, were designed and made by Thomas Paty, whilst William Halfpenny designed the pews, now replaced, and the wainscotting. He also noted for the first time that John Wood had recorded John Strahan's death in the 1742 edition of his *Description of Bath* and that therefore William Halfpenny was probably the designer of the whole building, in spite of the fact that the contract was not signed until the main structure was complete, roofed and closed in. Since then, others have dismissed Halfpenny's claim and have plumped for John Strahan as designer, considering Halfpenny as incapable of producing a building of such quality.

BABINGTON CHURCH

It does seem that Halfpenny was better at writing about buildings than producing them but John Strahan had not previously produced anything comparable to Redland Chapel, either. Although not perfect, this is a very fine piece of baroque architecture without parallel in Bristol. There is, however, another edition of it deep in Somerset, at Babington, not far from Ston Easton. This has a fragment of lead on the roof with the date 1748 carved in it and the Rev. John Collinson recorded the date of its completion as 1750 in his *History of Somersetshire* of 1792.

Redland was one of the smallest churches built in Bristol in the eighteenth century but, comparatively, Babington is minute. The entrance lobby is also the belfry and measures less than two metres square. The body of the church is about five metres by 14 metres with a semi-circular apse/chancel of perhaps four metres diameter. The nave has a deeply coved ceiling just like Redland's and a semi-circular giant arch to the apse, whose half-dome springs from a cornice which wraps around into the nave, forming proto-pilasters for the arch. The cornice has an enriched cyma-reversa top above a deep plain fascia which is supported by a deep caveto decorated with acanthus leaves which spring from a boldly decorated bead at the base.

The half dome above the apse is divided into three segments around a central eye which has a three-dimensional white dove on a blue 'heaven' and a golden sunburst; the dove is apparently flying down to the altar. The giant arch is panelled on its underside and has seven marvellous windswept acanthus-leaved rosettes, framed with egg-and-dart moulding. An amazing reredos – so three-dimensional that it may be made partly of wood as well as plaster – forms a rococo centrepiece to the apse and consists of a great gilded sunburst around a blue heaven containing ten now naturalistically coloured cherubs' heads and wings which support a central dark-blue roundel with a small cross and the sacred initials I H S in what is otherwise an entirely pagan feature. Below, a vine, groaning with ripe black grapes and interwoven with ripened ears of wheat, is supported upon a pair of rococo brackets by two more cherubs' heads who offer additional support to the vine with one each of their wings. All the colours described are very recently applied and I have no evidence about any previous colour scheme.

Flanking the rococo display piece is a pair of rather sombre arch-headed prayer boards with white plaster egg-and-dart moulding frames and, as a relief from Exodus XX and the Lord's Prayer and the Creed, have jolly cherubs' heads, holding their wings tightly below them, to form the keystones. Below is a dado rail of wave-guilloche form almost identical to that at Redland. The altar table and the communion rail are of Honduras mahogany. The rail has twisted 'barley sugar' balusters and a handsome moulded polished rail of fine quality. The altar table is a stunning, highly sophisticated piece of furniture, made to fit its curved background. Its front edge is also curved, on the same centre, its sides are S shaped and its legs and framing are multicurved and vertical surfaces are of basket-weave pattern. This highly complex and expensive piece of furniture needs careful expert examination, but it was certainly made for its site and was probably designed by the architect of the church.

The nave is furnished with its original box pews in handsome and straightforward oak, and an elegant pulpit rises, on the left, above the vicar's family pew. It has a backboard crowned with an urn, pagan again, and with no tester. On the right is the squire's pew which has, above it opposite the pulpit, the one important monument in the church, in white marble: a *putto* supports a white marble scroll recording names and dates of Henry Mompesson and his wife and Mr Thomas Pacy and his wife. The putto and the scroll stand on a handsomely detailed casket on classical consol brackets. Behind the putto a 'streaky bacon' red marble pyramid cuts through the plaster cornice and reaches up to the ceiling. A pair of rococo heraldic badges complete the presentation. Comparison with one of the *putti* on the Hilliard monument in

Babington Church, Somerset

Babington Church: the chancel and west end

The chancel arch and half-dome, with the dove, descending

Babington Church: the Mompesson/Pacy monument

the Lord Mayor's Chapel in Bristol confirms that this must have been made by Thomas Paty although it does not appear to be signed.

There are two other carved details inside the church. They are the magnificent George II coat of arms over the west door and a neat baluster font in white stone. This last is very similar to two Paty fonts in Bristol and the coat of arms is of a quality that suggests a Paty hand at work.

Externally, St Margaret's Church at Babington is, as Pevsner put it Germanically, 'very lovably placed on the lawn, in front of the house'. In spite of its tiny size, it is immediately reminiscent of Redland Chapel. The box of the nave is about a half-size replica, complete with three semi-circular headed windows on each side with architrave, springings and keystones, as at Redland, but simplified and therefore better. At the east end, the apse is expressed plainly as a half-drum and dome. Its very functional basis seems to be enhanced by three seventeenth-century chest tombs that are arranged in regimental precision behind it. The west end is quite different from Redland. There is no great triumphal arch entrance or cushion frieze and pediment but a very basic open entry porch which rises up directly to the square tower from which the octagonal bell turret rises, with a stone dome above crowned with a stone pineapple rather than the gilded ball and cross of Redland.

Nothing is the same, and yet it is all redolent of Redland. The proportion and the balance seem exactly right and the quality of the carved work seems right too, as is the composition of the change between the square and the octagon at the bell turret. The masonry curve behind the urns that is so memorable at Redland, is not used here, because of the tiny scale, but the transfer between the two shapes is just as elegant.

REDLAND CHAPEL

The date of St Margaret's precludes any possibility of John Strahan as designer and, therefore, his involvement at Redland is less likely too. There seems to be little doubt that this was the work of Thomas Paty, who was designing and supervising the reconstruction of Ston Easton Park at the same time. It is not so easy to assign the design of Redland. Thomas Paty designed all the carved elements of the exterior of that chapel and virtually all of the carved woodwork and plasterwork, the font and altar table. William Halfpenny controlled the completion of the nave and failed to resolve the problem that Thomas Paty had posed by his detailing of the triumphal arch at the East End and his arcades at the West. Why did he not resolve it? It could have been that there was no means of resolution without making physical alterations to structure already in position, the result of decisions taken earlier in the contract.

Almost nothing has survived about the personality of any of the Patys. The only things we ever get about them as people appear in their obituaries when their talents and their honesty and their gentlemanly characteristics are

Redland Chapel: the tower, octagon and cupola

Redland Chapel: the entrance front

Redland Chapel interior: the west end

Redland Chapel: the east end, with chancel and barrel vault

Superb Thomas Paty carving in the chapel's reredos [photo: Gordon Kelsey]

praised uniformly as if they were all the same man. There does seem to have been a uniformity about them all that betokens quietness and efficiency and straightforwardness. Under these circumstances it does seem odd to suggest that Thomas ducked out of a problem of his own making in the spring of 1742 but it seems he did.

He was at that moment extremely busy, working flat out for John Wood at the Exchange at a critical moment when the building was at cornice level with two at least of the coats of arms needing to be made, the capitals of the giant order and the carved decorations of the space between the capitals urgently required and all this at the time the most important interior works at Redland were being demanded. We know that he asked his uncle James(1) to do one or more of the pilaster capitals for the Exchange. Thomas Paty was still in his twenties and he could well have been unable to cope with the important but relatively subtle difficulty of a failure in alignments on the interior at the Chapel. He might have actually suggested to Mr. Cousins that William Halfpenny, always short of work, could take on the supervision of the works remaining there and so avoid having to resolve the difficulty. On the other hand, it may be that he too was offered 10 guineas to finish off the building and declined to do so.

In many respects, Redland Chapel is a masterwork both outside and in. It was designed by the same hand and mind that made St. Margaret's at Babington, where the mind was more assured and mature. At Redland Thomas Paty was exuberant, youthful, untouched by the Palladian messages from John Wood and Isaac Ware, and liable to the mistakes of youth. On the west front, the semi-circular lunette in the pediment, the segmental headed doorway and the niche with the shell hood over it, the giant Ionic order pilasters and the cushion frieze, all hark back to the last generation except that they are all assembled in a masterly manner of which that generation was not capable. Then, the tower and cupola reach a peak of flowery genius that nobody else achieved in Bristol in that century. The way the square of the belfry is translated to the octagon of the cupola via the draped vases and the concave splay behind them is perfectly beautiful, but above the cornice, which is emphasised with consols at the angles, the dome provides the uniquely brilliant finishing touch with a heavily gadrooned lead surface that leaves one breathless with admiration.

Inside the Chapel, the west and east ends produce the problem that Thomas Paty did not resolve. The west end is a logical restatement of the west elevation, with the segmental-headed doorway repeated and set in a three-bayed, two-storey arrangement that emphasises the vestibule, vestry and baptistry layout of the plan with a three-bayed gallery over it. Unfortunately, the springing of the arcade arches at the first floor do not relate to the springings for the semi-circular heads of the side windows, which, in their turn, do not line up with the springing of the triumphal arch that is the main feature of the east end. If the windows had been of a different size or at least had been relocated, the problem might have been partly or totally resolved. As it is, because of the unfortunate relationships the interior looks untidy, although the east arch and the tiny sanctuary shows Thomas Paty at his best. The sanctuary is a barrel-vaulted space which is coffered and stopped against the east wall with a lunette with an architrave surrounded by five plaster winged cherubs' heads which complement a swirling group of three, a 'glory' with intertwined wings which form the keystone of the architrave of the triumphal arch. This is at the top of a white painted Corinthian-order screen with full cornice. The cornice extends over the whole of the east end and is taken into and around the sanctuary, where coved corners disguise the rectilinear apse. Between the coves is the altar table and above it an eighteenth-century copy of Annibale Carracci's *The Embalming of Christ* and above that, the lunette, once glazed, which has been filled in and decorated since the war. The cornice, as it sweeps round, over the coved panels, provides bases for a pair of fully three-dimensional cherubs. The coved panels and matching panels to the north and south, the surround to the painting, the dado rail and the panelling below are in oak and are filled with gilded texts and are framed with the most magnificent carved limewood decorations consisting of cherubs' heads, ribbons, fruit, flowers, books, of the most astonishing quality. The dado rail is brought out of the sanctuary to form the base for the pilasters of the triumphal archway and it continues round to the west end, forming the cill to the windows, whose architraves are stopped with carved, winged cherubs' heads of the same splendid quality, good enough to have been once attributed to Rysbrack, but again by Thomas Paty.

In 1742, Thomas Paty was building up his workshop, establishing what was to become the most important element in the history of Bristol's architectural development in that century. In the space of perhaps two small houses and yards in Limekiln Lane, there would have been storage space and workshops for stone masons, monumental masons, carpenters, joiners and perhaps plasterers and even ironworkers. His own drawing office with maybe a shop or public space and his family life would have been enacted within this set-up.

In 1742, the business would have been under strain. He would not have been particularly thinking about his architectural status, so much as keeping his business functional and satisfying his clients. It would have been easy to retire from the role of architect at Redland, as his time would come later. Nevertheless, everything that we can see of Redland Chapel is by Thomas Paty. He was in every sense its architect, responsible for its glories and its mistakes. William Halfpenny was left in charge after all the decisions had been taken that fixed every architectural element permanently. Redland Chapel was Thomas Paty's youthful masterwork. By it, he won his 'spurs' as the most important Bristol architect of the century. In the last decade, after his death, he was beginning to be overshadowed by his brilliant son, though William did not live long enough to take over his mantle.

The exact date of William Hilliard's monument in the Mayor's Chapel is not known; but it is certainly from this first period of Thomas Paty's working life, when he was at his busiest and at his best, between 1740 and 1750. A likely sequence seems to have been Redland Chapel and the Exchange carvings, running together, Clifton Hill House and the Hilliard monument, the beginning of Park Street, St. Margaret's Church at Babington and a first phase of work at Ston Easton House. At this time he would probably have been wielding an axe and a chisel as well as a pencil. His workshop would have had few hands other than his own to start with and it is most likely that in this decade the links between the various Paty workshops were established. It was perhaps the regular income that came from his work on the Exchange that provided the springboard, not only for himself, but for all the Paty clan. By the end of the decade, he was a full-scale businessman, controlling an expanding organisation that would today have been called something like 'Paty Workshops Ltd.' By this time, he would have learned to delegate all his crafts skills except for drawing to his brother, cousins, nephews and employees.

CLIFTON HILL HOUSE

Clifton Hill House, the villa designed by Isaac Ware and built between 1746 and 1750 for Paul Fisher, was a very important project for Thomas Paty. Its influence on him as an architect was seminal. The Exchange, Bristol's most important Palladian building, was too ostentatious to serve as an exemplar for a young designer set to establish a local style. On the other hand, Clifton Hill House was a near-perfect English Palladian, low key, urbane structure that gave him all that he needed. It could even be suggested that this Isaac Ware house was the base from which Georgian Bristol sprang; at least, the Paty edition of it, for it was both elegant and remarkably plain, with decoration concentrated into one or two carefully composed and exquisitely executed flourishes. Not only did this suit the Paty temperament but it fitted with Bristol mercantile attitudes, too. Albemarle Row, Park Street and Great George Street owe their genesis to this house. Paty was paid over £2,000 for the work he carried out there. It included the carved monogram on the western (street) pediment and the heraldic device on the garden front, the elegant stone and metal staircase, all the carved timber work and splendid fireplaces. Isaac Ware was not in Bristol supervising the building and it could well be that Thomas Paty was in control as site architect.

ROYAL FORT HOUSE

Again, Thomas Paty's role here was that of carver under Mr. James Bridges as architect. Unlike Clifton Hill House, the architectural quality is rather compromised and not as distinguished. The three elevations of the house (the fourth being the junction with the service wing, an older structure) are various; the north (entrance) side is of seven bays, with the centre three

Isaac Ware's Clifton Hill House, the garden front and (below)
Thomas Paty decoration [photos: John Trelawny-Ross]

Clifton Hill House: staircase by Thomas Paty [photo: John Trelawny-Ross]

Clifton Hill House: Thomas Paty fireplaces [photos: John Trelawny-Ross]

windows as a group, set forward. The first floor has semi-circular headed windows and the second has squarish windows with keystones and stepped voussoirs. At ground level the centre space has the front door with attached Ionic columns, a full cornice and a triangular pediment, all enclosing the door with semi-circular headed fanlight within an architrave onto Tuscan pilasters. Two windows flank the doorway and light the hallway. The side wings are plain and the whole elevation is crowned with a modillioned cornice and a parapet which is solid at the wings and open with a balustrade over the centre. The west front is of five bays, has a slightly projecting three-bay centre emphasised with a triangular pediment at the roof, its tympanum carved magnificently by Thomas Paty. At ground level a rustic wall accents the three semi-circular headed windows and the first floor fenestration carries triangular pediments and the upper floor has eared architraves. The south elevation has a large bay window as its central feature, rising through the three floors, rusticated at ground level and with a balustraded coping at the top. The flanking bays have Venetian windows at first floor level.

The variability of these three elevations is notable, particularly as window-heads do not always line up horizontally. It gives an unsettled character to the whole that is rather disturbing. Although each front is well composed, in *To Build the Second City* Tim Mowl allocates the three elevations to the three contending designers of James Bridges, John Wallis and Thomas Paty. Wallis and Bridges were the most unlikely co-operators, though, and it is perhaps more likely that one of them was instructed to incorporate elements of designs produced by all three.

Inside, the house, endowed with a simple, logical plan, is beautiful and Thomas Paty with the plasterer, Thomas Stocking his next door neighbour and part of the Paty set-up, created a series of rooms, hall and staircase that together make the finest eighteenth-century interior in the city. A weighty Roman Doric entrance hall with rococo flourishes gives way, via an arcaded corridor, to an astonishing staircase hall. The stairs themselves are a fine cantilever of stone around three sides of the cubic space. Each step is handsomely carved on the underside and supports a marvellous wrought iron S finished with a patera at each end and carrying fine gilded acanthus-leaf decorations. The stairs might have been contained in a plain or simply panelled box with perfect dignity, joined to the arcaded corridor behind the entrance hall with an eliptical archway and lit by a Venetian window at the half-landing, but the designer chose to let the plasterer loose to create a riotous tour-de-force of decoration with three-dimensional vines, populated with birds and squirrels and interspersed with rustic scenes with foxes, sheep, shepherds, shepherdesses, dogs and ducks. The riot is actually properly controlled by the staircase itself at the base and by a splendid modillioned cornice above. The whole effect is of a perfect rococo heaven which should, but never did, lead to more superb decorations at first floor level. The ground-floor

The Royal Fort: south front

The east and south fronts, showing a lack of integration

The Royal Fort: ceiling of the staircase hall

The Royal Fort: niche and plasterwork in the staircase hall

The Royal Fort entrance hall: Doric and Rococo

rooms provide this. The most important room is entered on the axis from the entrance hall. Here, the decoration is frankly Chinese rococo. The doorway itself is treated to a timber carved decorative arrangement that includes wreathed and banded slender Corinthian columns supporting serpentine scrolls that rise up to meet and enclose a landscape painting which then reaches beyond it to the cornice at the ceiling and to spread arms of beribboned swags over the whole of the scheme below. Other serpentine scrolling comes out from the capitals below the landscape picture, to form a sinuous pediment over the architrave. The fireplace, which is a calm and cool piece of marble with Tuscan columns, has a mantle of sheer effervescence and above it, to the left and right, carved timber sporting trophies of whips, fishing rods, guns and dead birds amongst oak leaf sprays.

This virtuoso work by Thomas Paty is as good as any carved wood decorations anywhere in eighteenth-century Britain. The ceiling continues the rococo theme which culminates in the centre with an almost fully three-dimensional flying eagle.

Thomas Paty was in charge of all and the decoration of the drawing rooms to the south, though Tim Mowl suggests that the client's wife was the driving force behind the work. It is certainly true that Paty was hardly ever as free and easy as he was here, and, whether he was guided or not by Mrs Tyndall, was at his most brilliant and most up-to-date. He must have been aware of the work of the 'mad' Mr. Lightfoot, designer of the exotic interiors of Claydon House in Buckinghamshire, although these were not to be created until 1765, five years after the completion of Royal Fort.

ARNO'S COURT

Built about 1760 and onwards to 1765, Arno's Court is the work of William Reeve, the wealthy copper smelter, Merchant Venturer (he was Master in 1765) and Quaker. The house, the bathhouse and the palatial 'Black Castle' stable block were built as his career peaked. In 1774 he was declared bankrupt and expelled from the Society of Friends; the complex of buildings was sold, including the joke City Gateway, designed to house sculptures of kings taken from Lawford's Gate and Newgate, since removed to the City Museum and now handsomely replaced in a good rehabilitation and repair exercise. The estate has had a chequered and sad history. The house is now isolated from the other parts by the dual carriageway section of the A4 to Bath. For most of the twentieth century, the whole area became a low grade industrial estate. What had been the most beautiful of the structures, the Bath House, became derelict whilst in civic ownership and was eventually demolished and its facade transported to a new life as a romantic folly in Clough Williams-Ellis's holiday village of Portmeirion. The Gatehouse mouldered and provided rooting material for buddleia and ivy and the Black Castle made shift as a transport workers' club. Now, a supermarket has arrived and tidied things up. The Stable Block, Horace Walpole's 'Devil's Cathedral' has a new life as the Black Castle, a pub and the Gatehouse, which seems to have survived literally unaltered and pristine, acts as an entry to both the supermarket and the pub.

The three buildings, the House, the Bath House and the Stable Block are or were distinctive examples of Georgian gothick design of great charm. The Bath House, now gone but with its facade recreated on an idyllic site, was demonstrably out of Batty Langley and very good of its type, whilst the 'Black Castle' is both very unusual in form and in materials, is a highly imaginative work and probably unique. It was designed as stables and coach house and offices, with some reception spaces, too. It was constructed of slag blocks made from waste from the copper works at Crew's Hole but with architectural embellishments made of Bath stone. The workaday character of the place was translated into a real tour-de-force. It was completed before 1766 when Walpole saw it and commented in a letter dated October 22nd, 1766 '– going into the town I was struck with a large Gothic building, coal black and striped with white; I took it for the Devil's Cathedral. When I came nearer, I found it was an uniform castle, lately built and serving for stables and offices to a smart false Gothic house on the other side of the road.' Tim Mowl interprets these remarks as disparaging, but Walpole was perhaps being unusually generous, and recognising a soul mate, not reacting against a challenger to his own Strawberry Hill.

James Bridges is usually suggested as the designer here, but I think this was another collaborative work with Thomas Paty. Bridges quit Bristol and returned to the West Indies in October 1763 in the middle of the building period and he would have been upset and deeply involved in the argument about the design for the rebuilding of Bristol Bridge, well before that time. I think that Paty was increasingly left in charge of all aspects of the design and production. In fact, the house, the first and least distinguished part of the design, is probably more Bridges than Paty, whilst the Bath House, the Stables and the Gateway are probably mostly, if not entirely, Paty. The differences between Royal Fort and Arno's Court can be demonstrated by a change in the relationship between the two men. At the Fort, Paty was out to show how well he could supply all of Bridges' needs for details of every possible character in order to produce solemn (north face) playful (south face) and correct/classical (west face) elevations and the exuberant interiors. At Arno's Court, Bridges must have been feeling close to defeat by Bristolian politics and the efficient and amenable Mr. Paty was perhaps his only support. As Bridges' career in Bristol foundered, Paty was there to take on the reins.

In a valedictory article to James Bridges in *Felix Farley's Journal*, the sorry history of Bristol Bridge was spelt out and his prowess as an architect was described in detail, but there was no mention of Arno's Court. Certainly, by 1763, Paty was in charge, dealing with a perhaps difficult and interfering client who was probably leaning over the drawing board, particularly at the

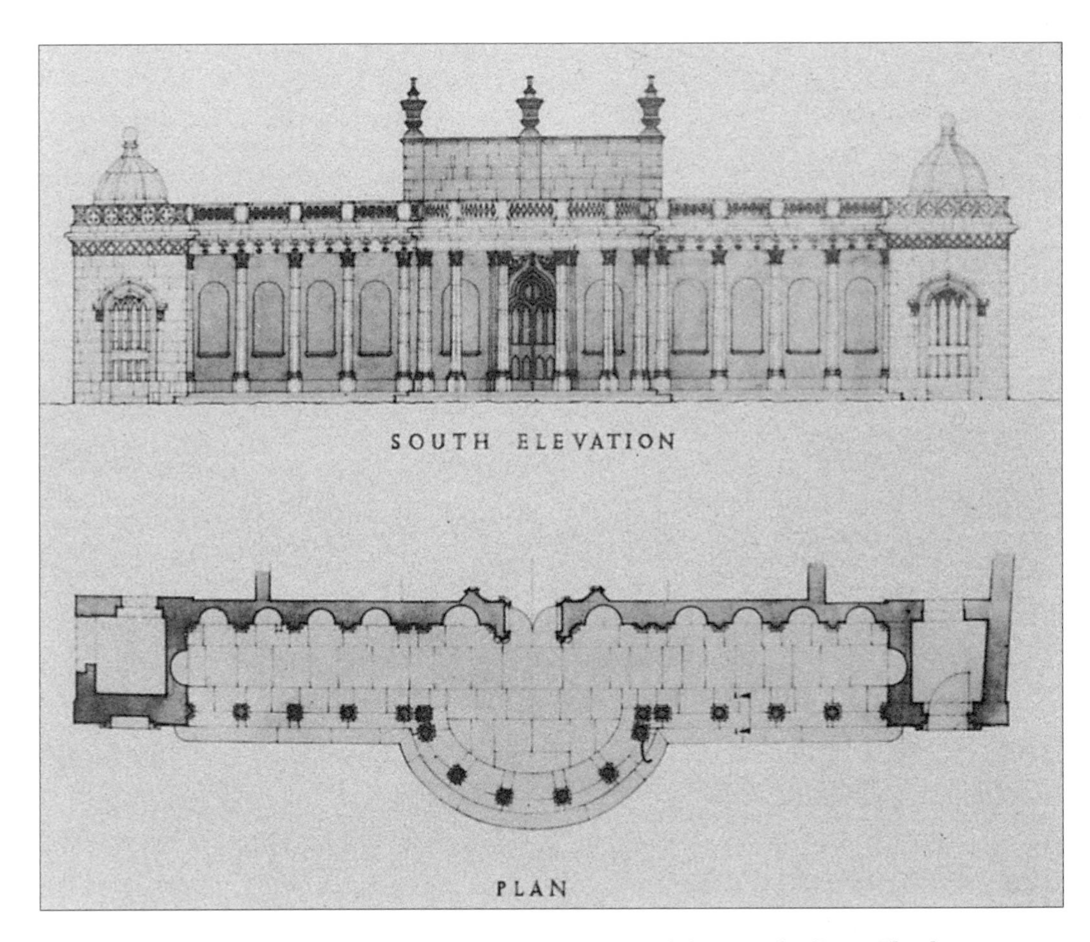

Arno's Court: the bath-house, from a measured drawing by Peter Floyd

Arno's Court: the mock City Gateway, with new casts of the statues of kings from the old Lawford's and New Gates of the City

Arno's Court: the stable block, 'the Black Castle', fronting onto the main road

In the courtyard

Arno's Court: the main front of the house

Arno's Court: entrance detail

time of the design for the Stable Block, when a more wayward imagination was at work than Thomas Paty normally revealed.

THEATRE ROYAL

Thomas Paty certainly spent a great deal of his time as a young man in subservient positions, overseen and sometimes controlled by others. His major work of the 1760s, the Theatre Royal, has the shadow of another hand, too. First, it is necessary to sort out whether his brother James(2) or he was in charge, because until recently, James was often credited. The evidence, simple and unequivocal, appears in a legal document where an assignment of a lease for part of the site of the theatre dated May 27th, 1765 stated that 'the Company of the Hoopers in consideration of the sum of one hundred and fifty pounds – have bargained sold assigned transferred and sett over – the said piece or parcell of ground – unto the said Thomas Patty for the rest of a term of 999 years in trust for the said Alexander Edgar, gent, William Jones, John Vaughan and Roger Watts, Merchants –' (members of the committee for building a theatre.)

If any doubts remain, the minutes of the first meeting of the committee resolve them. They were dated October 25th, 1764 and they read in part – 'that the building be immediately sett about under the direction of Mr. Thos Patty. That Mr Foote be employed as a mason, Mr Edward Crump as a carpenter and Mr Evans as a tyler, provided they will do their several works upon as good terms as others of their trade which is to be submitted to Mr Patty.' There are several other entries that demonstrate that Paty was to be in charge for collecting together the parts of the site from the several different ownerships into one unit for the new owners, and was to be in charge of organising the construction and for the overall accounting for the works. It is not, however, clear that he was to be in charge of the design work.

The late Bryan Little, writing in the Bristol and Somerset Society of Architects' *Journal* for September 1964, suggested that Paty was under the design guidance of 'Mr Saunders'. A little later, Miss Kathleen Barker in *The Theatre Royal, Bristol 1766–1966*, firmly stated that Thomas Paty was site architect and that the designer was the 'ingenious Mr Saunderson', the carpenter from Drury Lane. The minute book confirms this in the record of a meeting held on December 3rd, 1764:

> At this meeting were produced an elevation, ground plan and section of a Theatre drawn by Mr. Saunders, carpenter of Drury Lane Playhouse. Resolved to execute the Playhouse agreeable to the above mentioned plan as nearly as the circumstances of the ground will admitt.

The minutes are quite clear and imply a firm instruction to Mr Paty. It is unfortunate and surprising that no further minutes are recorded for the actual period of the building works.

A previous meeting, on November 6th, 1764 recorded that Messrs Edgar and Simmons had been to Portsmouth to finalise the deed of conveyance and then, being so near, had gone to London 'where they surveyed and took measurements of both the London Playhouses [and] they have a draft of Drury Lane and consulted a very ingenious carpenter, Mr Saunderson. They have collected such hints as they flatter themselves will be a means of saving some hundreds in building ye intended ho[use] in Bristol.'

This must have tied down Thomas Paty satisfactorily from the trustees' point of view, but the accounts for the building record that he was paid £200 for his work, a full 5% of the anticipated cost, the normal amount of remuneration paid to architects for a 'full service' although the final cost was nearly £5,000. Mr Saunderson had been paid previously the sum of £38.16.8 via Mr. Greene, one of the proprietors, on June 4th, 1764; this was a fee for the drawings and a consultation. The drawings were not drawings of the Theatre Royal but were Mr Saunderson's drawings for Drury Lane, the ones that gained him the soubriquet of 'ingenious'. The ingenuity was a simple one, one that resolved most of the audience problems that English architects had failed to resolve. He threw out the giant order that had been *de rigueur* as a means of holding up the several levels of balconies and inserted smaller, single storey columns instead, thereby reducing the massive blockages that had existed in nearly all theatres in England before. The single storey column had long since been used in France and Italy. It was this system that Mr Paty was asked to conform to. Perhaps the giant order at the proscenium enclosing the stage boxes was a Paty demonstration of independence. No drawings exist and alterations in 1800 and later mean that it is impossible to be certain about the appearance of the theatre in 1766 and how much it resembled Mr Saunderson's Drury Lane. Paty was paid a 'full service' fee, the committee was clearly satisfied with the work and Bristol businessmen were never over generous if not satisfied: in my view, Thomas Paty produced a design that incorporated Mr Saunderson's ingenuities, kept proper control of the craftsmen and worked to budget and to a timetable. In the fullest sense of the word he designed and built the Theatre Royal. Incidentally, Mr. Saunderson is not entered in Colvin's *Dictionary of English Architects* and he does not seem to have left any trace other than as 'the ingenious carpenter of Drury Lane'.

Alterations made to the auditorium in 1800 raise some question about whether the balcony support system was modified then. About £1,000 was spent, possibly enough to insert new columns as well as make the new gallery, the new ceiling and redecorate as well as to make some backstage improvements but it seems unlikely. There was a war on and prices were rising.

Mr Palmer, the theatre manager, in his description of the alterations said:

> The form was always admired by the best judges of that species of architecture. This form is still preserved but the additional boxes all round the

> front and the altitude given to the ceiling which was entirely new and considerably raised has so greatly improved the general appearance that it has all the effect of the London Theatres without the inconvenience of their too great magnitude. The decorations and ornaments are in the best style of elegant simplicity – the House is stone colour and the pannels a tender green with gold moulding and cornices; the columns that support the two rows of boxes are cabled with stone colour and gold alternately and have a light and beautiful effect.

This seems to suggest that the columns were new inserts although the previous statement that 'the form was always admired … [and] … is still preserved' does not. The new ceiling of 1800 may offer a clue here. It is not a tremendously sensitive piece of work, indeed it is rather vulgar in the way that would be expected a few years later, but it would have been much more punchy. This is tentatively vulgar, a bit uncertain. Some bits of the composition seem not to belong. These are the four strips of classical acanthus-leaved scrolling which are gilded on an apple green background. They match the gilded scrolls that decorate the Corinthian pilasters at the stage boxes and look more in tune with 1760s than with 1800s design. They look arbitrarily placed up there and may possibly have been appropriated to a new life on the ceiling after removal from the auditorium.

In spite of this, my view remains that the auditorium support system, with its single-storey columns, dates from 1766 in the hand of Thomas Paty and that if the odd acanthus strips on the ceiling were salvaged, they came from changes made in the proscenium arch or from the original ceiling.

The late Ralph Edwards, the honorary architectural advisor to the trustees who saved the building in 1942, wrote in the *Transactions of the Bristol and Gloucestershire Archaeological Society* that year:

> David Garrick … pronounced it to be the most complete of its dimensions in Europe … the interior which remains substantially unaltered was … the first semi-circular auditorium constructed in England. The builder was Gilbert Davis, the mason, Foot, the smith Franklyn and the interior decorations were carried out by Simmons and Michael Edkins, well known as a painter of Bristol porcelain and glass. The ceiling, still in perfect condition, probably dates from 1800. The actual structure of the theatre is unique and the only existing example which illustrates fully the peculiarly English features in stage development. The proscenium doors, the thunder run, the sloat system for raising scenery, the catwalks above the stage, the drum and shaft method of hanging scenery and the groove system, which obtained in every English theatre from the time of Inigo Jones until it disappeared about 1880; all remain together with traces of an apron stage. It is, in the opinion of experts, *the* historical theatre, par excellence, of England.

Although it may not be true that the ensemble of elements was uniquely English, the theatre as it existed then was certainly of unique importance. Since then, the building has not survived in the way that it should have. The back stage had been subjected to continuous change but of the cheapest and most superficial nature which, by luck and not judgement, left much of what was there before, *in situ* below the improvements. There can be no doubt that the advisors to the theatre company took absolutely the wrong decision when they decided, in 1970, to demolish the ancient theatre behind the safety curtain, in order to provide a late twentieth-century playhouse. The work then carried out destroyed a unique theatre that had been handed in trust to Bristol and the nation in the 1940s. The magnificent model of the theatre in its old form, now on display, which was given as a sop to the 'historicists', cannot replace what remained and was almost functional in 1970. It would have been difficult for the theatre company to have taken the alternative decision to restore the stage to a working eighteenth-century theatre, perhaps with modern facilities as well, but there is no doubt that their fateful decision destroyed half of the vital and ancient Theatre Royal. The City of Bristol now has an eighteenth and nineteenth-century auditorium in a modern theatre.

By the mid-1760s Thomas Paty was a very busy man. The years after the completion of the Exchange and Markets were particularly active with the projects outlined but he was also working on the new Bristol. In 1762 he was laying out Albemarle Row and, a year later, Dowry Parade. In 1763, he was concerned with Boyce's Buildings and, with his brother James, laying out and building the first houses in Park Street and soon afterwards, the brick and stone pavilions at the entrance to Great George Street. Bridge Street and King Square, St Augustine's Parade, Clare Street, the Butts and Denmark Street were all proceeding at about the same time, whilst the workshops of Thomas and his brother were turning out standard details for sale to other builders, producing fireplaces, doorcases, staircases and runs of moulding and, of course, memorials by the ton for churches in Bristol, Somerset, Gloucestershire and South Wales and for export too. Towards the end of his life, his sons John and William joined him and took some of the strain. The firm became 'Thomas Paty and Sons' in 1777.

Architecturally, the firm was dominant in Bristol. The influence was pervasive because, even when a Paty was not involved with the design, it was most likely that details came from a Paty workshop. In terms of design, it has been usual to accept that there was no reason to question its quality. Thomas Paty had a genius which he passed on to his son William and between them they made Bristol magnificent. Tim Mowl offers a different view. He starts his chapter on 'Bristol Under the Patys' in *To Build the Second City* by stating that 'mediocrity can be as potent a factor as genius in the development of a city. It was Bristol's bad luck to be dominated between 1760 and 1789 by the two

51 Park Street: the street's only surviving original doorway
[photo: John Trelawny-Ross]

Brick entrance pavilions to Great George Street [photo: John Trelawny-Ross]

brothers Thomas and James Paty' who, he said, 'exercised a generally stultifying influence on the city's architecture … Thomas was technically brilliant … as an architect he was equally unimaginative and conservative, devoted to brick despite being a stone carver.'

It can be agreed that in some respects at least, Thomas Paty was not a great architect, but Bristol may not have welcomed one and would certainly not have been comfortable with genius. Bristolian wealth was usually expressed rather carefully. It was important that buildings should not over-emphasise the brilliance of the designer or of the owner's wealth. This was a Quaker attitude and Thomas Paty provided exactly the proper image for it. Bristol's establishment was not universally Quaker, of course, but a cool simplicity and lack of ostentation suited Bristol merchants. It also suited their pockets, which tended to be fairly tightly buttoned.

Bristol's attitudes to building design were doubtless also affected by its close neighbour, Bath, whose chief protagonist had designed the Bristol Exchange. In 1741, John Wood had been put in his place when he tried to persuade the Committee for the Building to accept an 'Egyptian Hall in the Corinthian Order of eighty feet square, with a nave of fifty feet cube …' as the main focus of the Exchange. Instead, they demanded and got the cheaper 'small peristyle to comply with the opinion of the Citizens' who were 'startled with the Novelty of a covered place to meet in on Mercantile affairs.' Wood had got his way on the main form of the building and it was a triumphantly successful Palladian building, quite ostentatious enough to demonstrate Bristol's supremacy and not therefore needing to be repeated.

Thomas Paty's brilliance lay in his capacity as a facilitator. It has not been appreciated how much the Paty workshops controlled the production of domestic building in Bristol, particularly in the second half of the century. It is very difficult to separate out 'Paty' from 'not Paty' during this time and the vast majority of Bristol buildings constructed between 1765 and 1800 might well have contained elements derived from Paty pens and, more particularly, from their workshops. Thus it was that the only names attached to many Bristol developments are those of the contractors who produced buildings that seem to be (and actually are) Paty designs. Some are 'reach-me-downs' with a hotch-potch of stone-dressed details not well disposed, but in other cases, the elements are assembled with control, so that the result is a Paty design in the full sense.

As to Paty's tendency to use brick with stone dressings and for the use of Gibbs surrounds to doorcase and windows, brick with stone dressings need not be despised. Indeed, it was very much a metropolitan material, the stuff of which London had been and was still being made. Bristol brickwork was then truly magnificent and, perhaps crucially, it was positively not Bath. Thomas Paty had started his career under John Wood on the Exchange where he was fully aware of the rivalries between the Bristol and Bath masons: rivalries

Prospect House, Clifton Green

The Georgian House, Great George Street, 1790 [photo: Gordon Kelsey]

Charlotte Street [photo: Stephen Morris]

Albemarle Row: the centre house.
[photo: John Trelawny-Ross]

A corner of Hope Square

Hope Square: brick simplicity

Dowry Parade, Hotwells

Dowry Parade doorcase

Boyce's Buildings, Regent Street, Clifton, with a 1990s reconstruction on the right

that grew into hatred. In these circumstances, it is a wonder, perhaps, that he used Bath stone at all. In fact, he used it frequently, as the Bristol tradition by then was to use both brick and freestone.

The tendency to use 'old hat' design details like the Gibbs surround might be a reflection of Bristolian conservatism but it could also be good business. The detail is one that allows large effect with small labour, with one half of a detail being plain dressed stone and the other carved. This could be a useful detail to produce in quantity for sale to small builders. Thomas Paty did indeed tend to over-use a detail whose heyday had been in the forties, but he was in control, in a way that usually produced a building that was both sophisticated and straightforward. In any case, 'Gibbs surrounds' remained in use in London domestic architecture well into the 1770s.

Paty's capacity as a facilitator is also exemplified by another characteristic Bristol feature that he polished into a Paty signature. This was the stepped facade to accommodate the Bristol hillsides. Park Street is the best known of these and here the method was most developed, with pilasters between each three-bayed house, from ground to parapet: plain to separate the rustication of the entrance floors and to emphasise the cornices of adjacent houses as they wrapped around them to give a double enrichment at the top, shared between neighbours, the equivalent of a carved capital, and most cheaply achieved. The elegance of this solution is hardly noticed now among the jumble of shop fronts. Elsewhere, the stepped arrangement was less noticeable usually but is carefully detailed in Charlotte Street and in Berkeley Square.

The long building history of Park Street stretched from the 1740s to 1800 and beyond but Thomas Paty's standard design was used throughout, the only exception being the houses on the entrance to Great George Street that were designed as an accent to promote the special grandeur of this most important area. These were designed by Paty, too, and were built in brick with stone dressings and are pedimented on their Great George Street elevations. The windows have Gibbs surrounds at the upper levels and with the splendid quality of the brickwork they do indeed make a proper emphasis to the new street.

In 1762 Thomas Paty was also advancing on Clifton from another direction, in Albemarle Row. With Park Street as his guide, he did not think it necessary to demand a platform to raise a palace front but was happy to allow the terrace to express the contours of the site. In any case, he was not able to negotiate the finance for the complete terrace at the beginning and it was to develop piecemeal, although under single architectural control. The middle house, No. 5, had the centre three bays of a five-bay unit, pulled forward and accented with long and short quoins and at the top a pediment and a carved medallion of the land owner's initials. With careful detailing and meticulous craftsmanship, Paty produced a building group of great dignity and power. A year or so later, he was almost certainly involved in Dowry Parade, where almost the same formula was used but on three as well as five-bay houses with the same

Gibbs doorcases, the same stepped voussoirs at the window heads and the same channel-jointed pilasters, although the five-bay houses have since been divided and the doorways replaced. This is probably an illustration of Paty as supplier of materials for another builder, who set his own, rather dated, moulded sash boxes into the Paty window openings.

At about the same time as these Hotwells developments, Thomas Paty was also building on the hill in Clifton itself on Clifton Green and further north at Boyce's Buildings with another series of Gibbsian surround windows, both set boldly forward of the brick facades to give strong shadows and supported at the bottom with corbels, except at first floor where a string course replaces them.

In 1760, Kingsdown too was beginning to be developed but Thomas Paty does not seem to have been involved in the layout here nor in the design of many individual houses. George Tully was the designer. There are distinct differences in style and quality which are worth examining, as they apply to Brunswick Square as well, which was developed later in the same decade.

In most, if not all, Paty houses there is a distinct difference between solid and void with the space between windows being usually greater than the space of the window opening. This gives a noticeable feeling of solidity and calm. Paty seems never to have used his stepped voussoirs over a segmental window head. To combine the two details of equal mass to void with the segmental-headed, stepped voussoirs in King Square and in Brunswick Square is to produce a thin and restless result. Thomas Paty would not and did not make thin or restless buildings.

In Thomas Paty's later years he continued to be as active as ever. Park Street, Berkeley Square and Crescent, Bridge Street, Denmark Street, College Street and Charlotte Street ensured that there was a continuing turnover for the workshops in Limekiln Lane and in Horse Street. He was also architect for several country houses and the number of memorial stones provided was considerable. In 1777 he took his sons John and William into partnership when they were 23 and 19 respectively. There was no immediate evidence of a change in direction or in design quality and it is not easy to tell the difference between Thomas and William as designers, even after William took over at his father's death. William used more modern, neo-classical details that mark out his work from his father's but, always excepting Christ Church, the change was a seamless one. It is the same with the drawings in the copy-book where it is more or less impossible to tell the difference between them as draughtsmen.

Just before the end of Thomas's life, William (possibly with John) was in charge of a number of projects in Great George Street and Charlotte Street and more notably the rebuilding of Christ Church, City. In this church, William was to demonstrate his own quality as designer just as Thomas had in Redland Chapel nearly 40 years previously. In Great George Street, however, Thomas remained in charge even after death. There is a difference between

Christ Church exterior [photo: John Trelawny-Ross]

No.s 3 and No. 7 which probably marks the time of Thomas's death in 1789 but No.s 7, 23 and 25 epitomise Thomas Paty's philosophy of architecture exactly and they and the others in the group of seven mansions stand as his memorial. They are simple to the point of being stark. The ground floor is marked with rustication and the windows have voussoirs. The doorcase has Tuscan pilasters and a broken pediment to allow a semi-circular fanlight over the door; a plain platband caps this and stops all decoration thereafter, until, two storeys up, the cornice and plain parapet complete the statement. No emphasis at the edge, no pediment, no decoration at the windows, nothing. The house stand as an absolute statement of intent: an anonymous screen to the lives of wealthy merchant families. It states only the quality of the masonry, which is perfect, and simplicity and honesty.

It is a nice point whether this demonstrates a lack of imagination on the parts of owner and architect or, on the other hand, the ultimate perfection of an architecture meant to express Voltaire's philosophy and the revolutionary zeal of the young Coleridge, Wordsworth and Southey who might have met in No. 7 during the 1790s. There is no suggestion that either Thomas or William Paty had any thoughts on revolutionary poets, French or English, but they designed in a way that connected with the attitudes of the new generation of Bristol Merchant Venturers who were not unaware of what was going on in the literary world.

At Christ Church, the interior seems to be entirely by William but the tower and spire, the only part of the exterior that shows, is more old fashioned and Gibbs-like in detail, and, I suggest, was designed partly by Thomas. The entrance door was altered in the 1880s when the simple semi-circular doorcase was recut in a heavy, inappropriate neo-Florentine manner although the impact was minimal, unlike the introduction of the new reredos, in the same style, inside the church. The lower levels are only visible in Broad Street and consist of a ground level for the entry and an upper level for the clock face and the carved figures and bells made by James(1), removed from the previous building. Above this is a deep, stepped plinth on which sits the first level that presents four faces to the world. Here a double Ionic order of pilasters is capped with a full cornice and triangular pediment on each face. At the centre of each facade is a bold blind arch with a blocked architrave. The next stage repeats the stepped plinth so that the tower is noticeably narrowed by the time the top storey is reached where there is another double pilaster order, this time Corinthian and closed up so that the outer pilaster stands over the inner pilaster of the lower level. This allows the corners to be of plain, undecorated stone to form a firm base for the majestic urns at the angles, above the cornice and the parapet, whilst the pilasters and their cornice zone are stepped forward to emphasise the root of the octagonal spire above it. The spire actually starts with a vertical panelled turret, capped with a cornice. Above this the spire proper begins, divided into three storeys with strongly decorated bands and with oval openings on each face of the lower two levels. The final level is capped with a great gold ball, a wind vane and a cross.

This is the finest eighteenth-century tower and spire in the city and the last to be built. It makes a splendid culmination to the City scene, complementing the tower and cupola of the earlier All Saints nearby.

Of other important buildings in the city, constructed in the last decade of his life, the rebuilding of the Infirmary and the refacing of the Merchants' Hall are the most significant. Bristol Infirmary had been developed on its Marlborough Street site in the 1730s, first as an adaptation from an old brewery, then, in the 1740s, there was a replacement building, probably by George Tully, which was again rebuilt in 1784–6 by Thomas Paty. Although it is overlaid by alterations, this building is still recognisable today. It is an eleven-bay, three-storey block with a pediment over the centre five bays, which are set forward. The end bays are separated from projecting wings by a single-bayed recess with Venetian and thermal windows in each. The thin, three-storey wings project forward on the north front, sufficiently to define an entrance space separate from Marlborough Street, whilst on the south they projected to enclose a courtyard. The building looks more 'Charity Universal' than it did in its render on top of the original brickwork but it was always a basic, rather sombre structure, suited to its purpose and to Paty himself. The design took many years to come to fruition with the final building stage, which was the west wing, not completed until 1811, twenty-two years after Thomas's death and eleven after his son's. Some parts of the Georgian interior survive, including part of the staircase and the board room.

At about the same time that the Infirmary was being built, the Merchant Venturers were rebuilding their Hall in Marsh Street and King Street and Thomas Paty was designer. Photographs of the building, which was destroyed in the Second World War, are quite rare. It was not a building that attracted much notice, again in accord with the Merchant Venturers' philosophy. There would have been no reason why Bristol should not have had a sort of Bruges Halles or the Ypres Cloth Hall except that this was simply not the style of Bristol merchants. A small drawing in the Copy Book was for a simple and dignified new entrance front to the hall but the Merchants clearly wanted their existing building no more than smartened up a little.

STON EASTON

Evidence for Thomas Paty's buildings outside Bristol is very thin, but he was certainly busy in Somerset and Gloucestershire and probably in mid-Wales. I have already described the chapel at Babington, where all the evidence is visual but reasonable and conclusive. In that context, I referred to Ston Easton Park that was being brought up to date in the 1750s and between 1769–1786.

Drawings in the British Architectural Library show the entrance front to a house now identified as Ston Easton in two or three variations, none of which matches the house as it was finally built, which has a third floor throughout whilst the designs show just a central third floor or none, and a full pediment and, in one case, a giant Ionic colonnade which is not on the house. There is also an elevation of the garden front with a partial plan of that side, with a full attic storey and pavilion ends emphasised with rusticated quoins and pedimented roofs. Again none of this happened. The east front of the building as it exists is built of rubble stone with rustic quoins, with segmental-headed pediments over the ground-floor windows and flat cornices over the first floor and with no attic floor. None of the drawings is signed or identified, but several have notes, letters or dimensions, which, when compared with drawings in the Paty copybook, identify the hand of Thomas Paty as do the drawings themselves, whose draughtsmanship and character are strongly similar. These allow a categoric view that the drawings were made by Thomas Paty and that he was designer of Ston Easton, Palladianised.

As built, the house looks like Thomas Paty at his most economical. On close examination, the front is revealed as stucco, except the entrance doorway, its columned surround and the attic floor over the main house. This front has always photographed badly because the render is a rather gloomy grey and has none of the liveliness that one expects from weathered stonework. The detailing is amazingly crisp and has survived far better than Bath stone would have. It may be that the mixture used was special and secret, perhaps a sort of Coade stone, lacking nothing but good colour. This front should be examined by a materials expert, both to identify what the render is and whether a really subtle colourwash could not be applied to enhance its now dour presence. Inside the front door, things are very different. Everything here is of the 1750s, almost two decades earlier, from a time immediately after Thomas Paty's triumphant interiors at Royal Fort in Bristol and before money worries had impinged on Hippisley Coxe's grand dreams.

The interior drawings are for the Saloon and they are almost exactly as the room was made. The doorway is the most important element in the design; the doorcase has an eared surround capped with a modelled classic head and bold draped flowers beneath the architrave of the entablature for a surrounding pair of $\frac{3}{4}$-round Corinthian columns that are shadowed by squared pilasters. The frieze over the architrave is a boldly carved Roman *fasces*, but the bundle is made up with oak and vine leaves, all crowned with a cornice and pediment, modillioned. This appears to be of carved wood and not plaster. The picture frames that flank the doorway again are very bold and probably all of wood, with a large shell at the top supported by rococo brackets, and the sides and base enriched with bold festoons of flower drapes. They contain a pair of rather boring grisaille representations of covered urns. The drawing actually shows a ghostly pair of classical landscapes that would have been much more interesting.

Ston Easton: drawing of the entrance front

Ston Easton: drawing and photographs of the saloon

Ston Easton: entrance front and one of the pavilion ends

The entrance door with Roman Doric colonnade and entablature

The fireplace wall, which is against the old house on the north-west, has a bold and simple fireplace with a pair of free-standing Tuscan columns supporting an architrave and a deep frieze with an oval patera on it. Above the column, the frieze runs over the fire opening, quite plain until it meets a large central panel with a carved quiver of arrows, crossed with a bow, encircled by a laurel wreath. The whole panel spreads over the architrave and the lower part of the cornice above it, which forms the mantlepiece, stepping forward over the columns. Above all this is a grand, pedimented picture frame which reaches almost to the cornice of the saloon. The frame is eared at the top, has an egg-and-dart outer edge, except at the bottom where it sits on a Thomas Paty favourite Greek fret, making a clear demarcation between the fireplace and the overmantel. The cornice has a double row of little modillions under more egg and dart making an unusually rich detail at the top, above a frieze which consists of a pair of triglyphs at the outer edges that seem to be three fishes standing on their tails, enclosing decorative motifs that act as a precursor to the main cornice with a pair of shells and decorative leaf forms. At the centre, flanked by the shells, is a plain, undecorated plaque.

The window wall has the architraves around the windows sitting on bracket ends onto the strong dado rail; the other wall has a pair of doorways with eared architraves, and an amazing detailed and shaped frieze below a cornice that matches the overmantel. Between them is a handsome niche recess, now supporting a bust of William Pitt the Younger, who had some association with the house. Above all is the cornice which starts with an architrave and frieze which has a powerful motif of huge shells linked with bold scrolls and fruit swags, again so strongly modelled that they could be of wood rather than plaster. All this is topped with a splendid modillioned cornice and, in the centre of the ceiling, a great eagle comes away from the sun in an oval.

The saloon is a Thomas Paty masterpiece, as good as the best of the work at Royal Fort. The other rooms, the Yellow Dining Room, the Drawing Room, the Library and the Print Room all have (in the drawing room, *had*) fine fireplaces, the Library with a beautiful overmantel and classical picture, fine cornices and dados. The library also has a marvellous set of bookcases and the print room has a pair of splendid once glazed recess cupboards, all designed by the architect. All this work was first phase, of the 1750s.

In November 1997 Mr Antony Woodward described, in an article in *Country Life,* how the entrance front was made symmetrical by the addition of the flanking wings and pavilions as a last phase, built between 1769 and 1786 by John Hippisley Coxe's son, Richard, but there is an inter-relationship between the 1750s interiors and this final phase that cannot be denied. The fenestration of the Print Room, the Library and the Yellow Dining Room all must have appeared onto the Entrance Front then, together with the new entrance doorway and surround. These must have been cut through pre-existing rubble stonework or made new in the same material. Clearly the final design must have been available then. Whether a decision had already been made to finish the building by rendering the detail is not known, but no ashlar seems to have been used other than on the entrance way, and, rather unexpectedly, on the attic storey. The mystery is unresolvable but it must demonstrate that there were difficulties and perhaps arguments between the architect, the builder and the client. Thomas Paty will have made his grand Hippisley Coxe coat of arms and flourishes in Bath stone and his roof decorations, too, so it would have been easily agreed to allow the rest of that part of the building to be made in ashlar. For the rest, Thomas was probably not on site often enough to prevent corner-cutting decisions being taken by his client, already half mad, perhaps.

A pair of drawings in the British Architectural Library collection warrant description at this point. They are marked 'East side of Drawing Room – Coxe Esq.' and 'Chimney side of Drawing Mr Cox Park Street'. They show the two long sides of a room with a handsome fireplace and a rather tentative design for a classical wall mirror; the handwriting is quite definitely that of Thomas Paty and the room depicted is of a first floor room on Park Street in Bristol. Because of the location of the drawings, Mr Cox(e) was either John or, more likely, Richard Hippisley Coxe of Ston Easton: further and final confirmation that the other drawings were by Thomas Paty.

Although Somerset was probably Thomas Paty's birthplace and where he might have felt most at home, he almost certainly spent more time designing for Gloucestershire gentlemen. Nicholas Kingsley, in *The Country Houses of Gloucestershire* Vol 2, says that 'During the 18th century, the main centre of building skills on which Gloucester gentlemen drew was Bristol. Close ties between Bristol and Gloucester tended to exclude the often more sophisticated architects of Bath.'

In 1750 Thomas designed the small octagonal room called the Waiting Hall at Badminton for the Duke of Beaufort. It stands effectively and with charm with its fine fireplace beside William Kent's work next door. This work at Badminton was carried out whilst Thomas and his brother James(2) were working on Stoke Park with Thomas Wright for the same client.

Two other houses at Alderley – the Grange, which bears quite strong similarities to the drawing for the Merchants' Hall extension in the Copy Book, and the Upper House there (now demolished) – are both suggested as possibly by Thomas.

BEACON HOUSE

Another house in Gloucestershire, at Painswick, was identified by Timothy Mowl in a *Country Life* article in 1997 as having interiors that must have been by Thomas Paty. I think that the house as a whole was by him, as was another, tiny palace of a house, a few hundred yards away in the heart of the town, which has a marvellous Palladian front and some delectable interiors.

Beacon House has a Palladian facade in five bays, with three storeys, a rustic ground floor with a grandly scaled Gibbsian doorcase, a *piano nobile* with tall architraved windows with blind balustrades below and with triangular and segmental pediments over, on the three central units, whilst the two flanking windows of the wings, which are set back, have no balustrades and have flat cornices. The attic windows are almost square and have simple architraves. The composition is completed with a modillioned cornice with a balustraded parapet over it.

All is pure Palladianism out of John Wood's Bristol Exchange and Isaac Ware's Clifton Hill House and might have been better than both in Burlingtonian correctness had it not committed the cardinal sin of a failure in symmetry. Although everything is meticulously correct vertically and all the elements properly shaped and ordered, the building is chaotic horizontally. Not only are the flanking outer bays unequal, but the central three bays are, too, so that the whole elevation is disastrously uncomfortable. In spite of careful detailing, it reads as a caricature of Palladianism. It is difficult to understand how such a terrible mistake happened unless the facade was a reconstruction of a pre-existing building, in which case a different, less formal arrangement might have worked better. Either that, or it is a dreadful illustration of the sort of disaster that can occur when an over-busy architect fails to visit a site with an impatient client and or a wilful builder.

Typically, Thomas Paty did not allow the disaster outside to affect his interiors which, once again, were very successful. His skill here is still apparent in spite of the fact that the dining-room ceiling and some of the fireplaces were shipped to America in the 1920s. What remains is the entrance hall and staircase hall which is in Thomas Paty's Royal Fort rococo style. It is less controlled, more boisterous and contains references to the god Pan and a local satyric cult which links the house and its decorative scheme to Painswick House itself. This is another mid-eighteenth century house with uncertain design attribution but with Bristol connections. David Verey in the Cotswolds volume of the *Buildings of England* series, offered John Strahan and William Halfpenny as possibilities. If it is of the 1730s then it is possibly too early for Thomas Paty, who was only 17 in 1730 but, by and large, the garden works are later and they could easily have been by him.

Before moving on to his son William, it is worthwhile attempting an assessment of Thomas's architecture and asking questions about his aims, professionally. This last is significant because one of the few certain facts about his life in Bristol is that he never became a member of a craft guild and was never elected a freeman of the City. This extraordinary fact about the most successful local building craftsman of his time seems not to have been discussed before. Local byelaws prohibiting anyone not a freeman from exercising a trade or opening a shop in the city had been in existence since 1696 and probably enshrined a long previous history. A fine of £5 a day for those who did not comply was raised to £20 a day in 1703. Latimer says that 'the authorities acted capriciously in the matter' and Thomas Paty seems never to have been challenged or fined, nor was he discriminated against. Indeed, the Corporation consulted him regularly as an architect and employed him as a stone carver and as a mason. The byelaw was designed to protect locals against foreigners in a time-honoured way, but the system was beginning to break-down by then, particularly with the emergence of professional architects. The practice was breached comprehensively by John Wood and his Bath freemason, William Biggs, in 1740 with the building of the Exchange. It is interesting that Thomas Paty was employed as stone carver on that contract. He was much impressed by the Bath architect, who was not much older than he and was polished, gentlemanly, talented, amazingly successful, and demonstrably 'above' trade but hand-in-glove with tradesmen and craftsmen. The concept of being 'above trade' was an important element in Paty's dream from then on and it ensured that he would not join the Bristol 'club', and become a freeman. In fact, however, the workshop was and would remain the centre of his life. If one examines his actions at the other end of his career over his sons' education, the dilemma that he created becomes clear.

John and William's education in sculpture and architecture were circumscribed by their father's needs for his practice and workshop. He wanted his sons to have the advantages that contact with the metropolitan world could give but he was not interested in their stepping out beyond the realm that he had already constructed for them. The Paty workshop was his creation and it gave him, and would give them, effective control of the Bristol building scene, influence throughout the south-western province and, via the Port of Bristol, in Wales, Ireland and even, surprisingly, the West Indies and North America, too. They could build up from a very sound foundation and would have no need to break in on London to make their fortunes. Thomas Paty's refusal to join the Bristol freemen meant that he had to send his sons away for their education, which would separate them, too, from their Bristol fellows. It is extraordinary that there is no evidence or commentary about what must have been a very rare situation. Paty required his peers to recognise him as a professional man, outside the trade guild system, whilst his workshop shone out above everyone else's and he grew to be a rich man by it. At the beginning of the twenty-first century it is impossible to understand how this would not create jealousy amongst his mason contemporaries, or prompt some comment that would have been reported in the local press. Nothing has come to light.

Both John and William, however, became freemen. John was entered, as an architect, 'admitted to the Liberties of this City for that he married Elizabeth, daughter of William Perry, Mariner, deceased, and hath taken the oath of obedience and paid £0.4.6.' on April 22nd, 1789, just twelve days before Thomas Paty's death. William was more tactful and waited until December 9th, 1790 when he was admitted on the payment of a fine of 15 guineas for those who have no entitlement through parentage, apprenticeship or marriage to a burgess's daughter.

Thomas's will was signed and witnessed by all three of his children *after* John had become a burgess. It was in fact dated May 2nd, 1789, just days before he died. The wording implies that there might have been a coolness between Thomas and his eldest son, as his wife's existence is not recorded whilst William's Sarah and Elizabeth's husband Thomas King of Bath are both referred to. It may be that John's decision to 'become a tradesman' had pushed the old man into his final illness, but the document shows a family united, paying allegiance to their father as he lay dying.

For his compatriots, Thomas Paty was a leader who could do no wrong. Timothy Mowl has questioned this received wisdom – that Thomas was *the* Bristol architect of the eighteenth century – suggesting that he was timid, old-fashioned and mediocre; that he and his brother James served Bristol ill, that he boringly built in brick whenever he could, rather than Bath stone, and that he harked back to Gibbsian detail in an 'old-hat' manner. It is true that Thomas often used Gibbsian detail as a trademark, and he often chose to build in brick with Bath stone details. The Bristol bricklayers indeed were marvellous craftsmen and Thomas and they believed that they were building in an up-to-the-minute and metropolitan manner, as indeed they were. London brick terraces were going up all through the City and the West End during the last decades of the century. London stocks were perhaps more characterful than the Bristol and Bridgwater bricks used here, but they had the same amazing skills in jointing and pointing. Bristol eighteenth-century brickwork has often survived the nineteenth and twentieth centuries better than its Bath stone equivalent.

A Paty brickwork terrace is as worthy if not more worthy than a stone one. Paty's Bristol works were almost entirely domestic and, essentially, modest. His work was invariably carefully detailed, carefully proportioned and well mannered. When he was able to build expensively, as in Great George Street, he eschewed visual fireworks and did what he did normally, but better, so that, although anonymous, it was often a masterpiece. The simplicity and austerity of Paty facades frequently screen interiors of great exuberance. Both Thomas and William gloried in masking a flamboyant interior with a calm and simple exterior.

The essential design differences between the father and son have not previously been clearly understood because of uncertainty about their individual contributions over the period between 1777 and 1789. In fact, Thomas seems to have shared the design load with the boys in the monumental business as soon as they came in but on the architectural side, he stayed in charge until almost the end. It was not until 1786 that he gave over control sufficiently to permit William his first major and significant design job on the interior at Christ Church.

It may be possible to trace design characteristics that are specifically typical of Thomas and William which allow some level of agreement on their individual contributions, although the possible interventions of Thomas's brother James and William's brother John ensure that the 'waters remain muddied'. Tim Mowl identified the tendency to Gibbsian detail, which has the mouldings of a window or door opening interrupted by a block of plain stone projecting beyond the plane of the surround at every other stone course, as a characteristic Thomas detail. He also suggests that James Paty(2) was the Gothicist who was responsible for Arno's Court Bath House. None of this adds up to any real individual and recognisable characteristic that ensures that a work is by one or other of the Patys. If one thing comes through, it is a proportional integrity that is invariable and immediately recognisable. This standard can be seen on every one of Thomas Paty's domestic elevations in Bristol and is not replaced in Paty work until the metropolitan-inspired neo-classical work of William appeared.

At his best, Thomas Paty was a really good architect; on the south front at Royal Fort for instance, and on the tower and spire of Christ Church and in his stunning interiors, but at the end of William's short life, it had become apparent that he was much the better of the two. On the whole, Thomas's imagination was limited by his continuing 'busyness' which never allowed time for pause and consideration to think about the future of architecture. His decision to send his sons to the Royal Academy for their education was an advanced one but he made no attempt to allow William, at least, to carry on for more than a year or to push him on to Rome afterwards, then the proper finishing school for aspiring architects. It is probably true that Mr. Paty's sons only wanted to get back from London to show their mettle on the Bristol scene, but this would have reflected their father's inadequacies. He saw his future and theirs contained within the boundaries of his own parish, although he and they were capable of stepping way beyond it.

In fact, the system that he had devised for himself and his sons was in some ways unique. It revolved around the workshop or, rather, the family of workshops. His skill as a designer informed the craftsmen in stone carving, joinery, plastering, iron working and plumbing who were his employees or associates. In this way, he was able to supply all the design and detail of the whole work as a sub-contractor to an anonymous mason or bricklayer contracted to the client. In this way, his profit was guaranteed, his risks were minimal and he remained in charge of the design. Sometimes he was architect, officially instructed. Then he would be in control of the finances and of the masons and bricklayers, but all the other skills would usually be provided by his own employees and associates as before. In this case he would take two profits, but the work would be harder and he would reckon to have earned the extra.

Thus it was that when John and William returned from their London experience, they stepped into a business that was controlling Bristol's building industry. It is not clear whether Thomas and William ever acted as entrepreneurs, using their own money to promote the many projects that they worked on. They probably did so only rarely. Certainly, it is clear that William was not embroiled in the Clifton fiasco in 1793. The workshop arrangement would have allowed him to survive with profit whilst the masons and bricklayers actually building the properties succumbed. This was the essence of the Paty system, which was the main characteristic that passed between the two men at Thomas's death. His contemporaries accepted and trusted his ways which were considered to be absolutely honest. The obituary which appeared in *Bonner and Middleton's Bristol Journal* for May 9th, 1789 left no doubt:

> Monday died in the 77th year of his age, Mr. Thomas Paty, architect, whose extensive virtues, professional abilities and strict integrity, will in this City ever be rever'd, and, we may say, whose paternal affection added a lustre to his character. – Let those who Knew him, – those who loved him speak.

William Paty

From the summer of 1789 William Paty was in charge of his father's workshop, building yard and house in College Place. He was then about 32 years old and had been in partnership with his father and his brother for the last twelve years. In this year, the rebuilding of Christ Church was a major project, nearing completion; at the Infirmary, the central block was approaching completion, and No. 7 Great George Street was building. Park Street was slowly growing up the hill, as would-be owners or speculators found the money, while Berkeley Square and Berkeley Crescent and Charlotte Street were building, or about to start.

Deeds for buildings in Berkeley Square and Berkeley Crescent survive, which show how architectural control was maintained, without any mention of the controlling designer but with complete and detailed description of sizes and elements and materials to be used.

> In an agreement dated January 4th, 1791 for the construction of No. 6 Berkeley Parade [now Berkeley Crescent] between:
>
> | | |
> |---|---|
> | William Harland | |
> | Benjamin Tucker | House Carpenters. |
> | John Clement | Plumber. |
> | Mathew Mills Coates | Gentleman. |
> | of the first part | AND |
> | Robert Williams | Tyler and Plaisterer |
> | John Fisher | Accountant (Trustee of Williams) |
>
> and whereas the said William Harland, Benjamin Tucker and John Clement intend to erect and build or cause to be erected and built on the said plot – of ground granted and conveyed to them as aforsaid Seven Messuages or dwelling houses one of which is to be built by the said John Clements and is to be fifty feet wide in front at the south-east side next Berkeley Square and the other six of the said messuages are to extend from the north or the north-west front of the said messuage so to be erected by the said John Clement onto the said road leading to Clifton and the four centre houses are to be built in an elliptical or semicircular direction and the said six messuages or tenements together with the north front of the said messuage intended to be built by the said John Clement are to form

a regular pile of building which is intended to be called Berkeley Parade
AND WHEREAS
the said Robt. Williams hath contracted and agreed with the said William Harland Benj. Tucker and John Clement for the plot – of ground hereinafter particularly described whereon he intends to erect a messuage or dwelling house conformably to the said design laid down by the said William Harland Benj Tucker and John Clement and to an elevation indorsed on the back of these presents and which is subscribed by them the said Harland Tucker Clement and the said Robert Williams.
And also that the said Robert Williams – shall and will on or before the said 25th day of March 1792 at his or their own costs – erect and build and perfectly compleat one messuage or tenement or dwelling house with proper and convenient offices in and upon the said plot – in a firm good and workman like manner and that the front thereof next the said parade shall be built with the best front bricks and shall be well jointed and neatly executed with freestone coignes or pilasters of twenty inches wide with recesses made in the windows four inches deep at least and a freestone plinth course not less than ten inches wide. That the door shall have a freestone case with a fan sash and semi head. That the said house shall be five stories high including the garrets and kitchen floor and there shall be a double cornice and a parapet coped with freestone over the front of the said messuage and that the parlour storey of the said messuage shall be of the height of eleven feet in the clear That the drawing room storey over the parlour shall be of the height of eleven feet and a half in the clear and the attic storey shall be of the height of eight feet and a half in the clear with a curb roof over it allowing garretts therein and that the roof of the said messuage shall be roofed with the best Cornish tile as will the flat as the curb thereof. That each sash in the parlour and dining room stories shall be six feet and a half high and three feet and two inches wide clear of the frames and shall contain 12 lights of regular dimensions and each sash in the attic storey shall contain six lights of equal dimensions and shall be 3 foot and 8 inches high clear of the frames and shall be of the same width with those in the other stories that there shall be no window, building or frontispiece in the front of such messuage which shall project therefrom. That no lead or other pipes shall be brought from the top of the said messuage down the front thereof. That the said intended messuage shall be built in an uniform and handsome manner and altogether conformably to the strict rules of architecture and good workmanship and the front thereof shall be in every respect uniform and regular with the back fronts of four houses already built by the said Benjamin Tucker on the north east side of the said square and that no building except the said messuage – shall be ever erected on the said plot

> of ground already granted and that so much of the wall intended to be built on the south east side of the said ground hereby granted as is coloured green in the plan shall never exceed the height of seven feet but that pallisades may be set therein of the further height of 2 feet and that the said Robert Williams – shall – make an area or court of 6 feet wide in the clear before the whole front – next the said terrace or Parade and put a proper hard stone plinth on the pavement next the said area worked with a proper base moulding and on such plinth a neat iron rail in an uniform manner with the other buildings and also shall and will on or before the time appointed make a public footpath before the whole front of the width of 12 feet which shall be set in good brown lime.

There follow more detailed instructions on the layout of the terrace, instructions for drain laying, requirements for insurance and restrictive covenants that applied and which laid down amongst others that the house, when complete, should not ever be used as 'a public school for the instruction of youth or for the teaching of drawing or music.'

This long quotation from an eighteenth-century legal document demonstrates how the Patys were able to ensure the control of building tradesmen who were willing to build speculatively on their sites. The system is one which gives safety to the design concept whilst allowing the designer freedom from the risks of financial involvement. It is interesting to speculate on the links between Thomas and William Paty and the lawyers who drew up the documents.

Between May 1789 when Thomas died and December 1800 when William died the practice/workshop handled or organised the production of at least the following buildings: Christ Church, City, the New Infirmary, 7 Great George Street, 23, 25, 27, and 29 Great George Street, Charlotte Street, Park Street, Berkeley Square, Berkeley Crescent, Royal York Crescent, Cornwallis Crescent, Belleview, St Vincent's Parade, Portland Square, Prince's Buildings, Sion Hill, the Mall, buildings in Clifton Down Road, Gloucester Place and, at Henbury, the new mansion for Mr Harford.

THE BUILDING OF CLIFTON

Much of what we now recognise as Clifton was built or rather half built during this decade and much of William's reputation rests here. The Mall/Sion Hill and Prince's Buildings had been started in Thomas's time but William and his brother John must have been more or less in charge by then. The most important question about Clifton, however, is who invented the notion of the two contour-hugging crescents of Royal York and Cornwallis and who devised the stunning relationship between the Paragon and Royal York. How did a magical result emerge from a long-drawn out, painful and financially disastrous process? No drawings appear to exist and the whole development was started in a great surge described then as a mania, not the best condition for the production of works of art. In 1793 the surge collapsed; many of the speculators were left bankrupt and the majority of the buildings left roofless or otherwise incomplete. One person apparently unharmed by all this was William Paty, although he died just seven years later when he was 43 years old. Whether this was related in any way to the stress of these years, we do not know, but he died a relatively wealthy man, several years before the economic upturn that allowed the eventual completion of Clifton.

The one thing that is certain about Clifton is that no one invented its layout on a drawing board. If there was a controlling genius it was the genius of the place. This still exists and can be discovered by walking from Hotwells up Granby Hill. The virgin landscape of the Clifton hillside was marked with a track on the same site, twisting then as now, on the way to the summit to ease the way to the still steeply sloping plateau. This can be seen on a painting in Blaise House. The track was and is a young person's route, needing extra energy but the journey highlighted the positions of all the important building sites on the journey up, almost as clearly as now. It perhaps did need a practical genius to foresee the disposition of the several terraces and crescents and their relationships. That is the relationships between Windsor Terrace and the Paragon, the Paragon and Royal York Crescent and Royal York and Cornwallis Crescent and the last two with the older group of manors towards the wooded hillside of Clifton Wood. The magic of Clifton lies in this more than in architecture. The contours and boundaries and footpaths actually pre-empted many decisions but they had to be controlled; that controller was probably Thomas Paty, although he did not live to see much of it built.

The journey up the hill takes one first past the site of Freeland Place, which was in fact the last of the terraces to be developed in the 1820s and 30s, but it was there and must have been recognised for its potential from the first, then on past a number of pre-existing houses westwards to a ledge onto the Gorge which, with some judicious engineering, could be expanded to create the site for Windsor Terrace, then, to the right, the contour line of Cornwallis Crescent stretching almost to the distant Goldney House, then on to the great rock outcrop for the Paragon to crown the development, but behind it, Prince's Buildings and to the east the far more important vision of Royal York Crescent, already there as the footpath to the heart of the village at the Parish Church, nesting amongst the manors.

The sites were sufficiently identifiable in the landscape of Clifton for the result to be a foregone conclusion for anyone with the ability (or genius) to see it. Actually, Granby Hill itself, with Hope Chapel Hill, makes a contribution to this unique development. The group of houses that survive, following the curving line of the original footpath, ends in a tiny, boat-shaped house whose significance is vastly greater than its size suggests. It is the tip of an arrow-shaped development of building in Hope Square or Hope Triangle as it might better be called. A block of 1970s flats fills part of the site but, unusually, follows the form of the previous houses quite accurately. This strange design, in the shape of an inverted Y, is the most organically ordered piece of eighteenth-century building in Bristol and although compromised is not destroyed by the modern flats. It demonstrates how this part of Clifton was an inevitable product of patterns of ownership, contours and aesthetic requirements. The boundaries on the south and west were established from the footpaths and on the north and east by estate boundaries. The buildings followed these boundaries and then had to cope with the enormous contour differences across the site. The lowest levels are fifty feet below the highest on a site of less than two acres. Within this context a group of high density with good views, easy access and amazingly attractive form was created, which, at the top, at the boat-shaped cottage, seems to provide a fulcrum for the layout of the whole of the rest of the Clifton hillside development. Cornwallis Crescent and Windsor Terrace spring off from the metre-wide tip and the Paragon stands almost directly over it. The roofs of this little gem of a building have been altered recently and are now less boat-like so the effect is reduced, but it is still exceedingly important.

The whole of Clifton on the hill started in or around the last decade of the century. The Mall started at the beginning of 1789, Prince's Buildings were built between 1789 and 1796, St. Vincent's Parade, Hotwells was 1789–90, Windsor Terrace, 1789–1808, Royal York Crescent, 1791–1820, Cornwallis Crescent, 1792–1830, Saville Place. 1790–1810, Belleview, 1792–1815, Richmond Place and York Place 1793–1810, Granby Hill and Hope Square, 1790/91. The Paragon had been first designed in 1790 but did not commence until 1809 and was not completed until 1815.

Most of the sites were in the ownership of the Society of Merchant Venturers who were well to the fore in granting leases to speculators and, if not the promoters of the building mania, were very much acting as midwives. The declaration of war between France and Britain in 1793 was the reason for the collapse of confidence. After this, there were apparently more than five hundred unfinished houses in Clifton and the city. Walter Ison quotes from James Malcolm, an antiquary, who wrote in 1807: 'I do not recollect a more melancholy spectacle than a walk on a dull day through the silent and falling houses in the western environs of this City [where they seem to] represent deserted streets occasioned by a siege or ravages of a plague.'

The scheme for Clifton was mapped out by the ground itself, the pre-existing routes across it and the ownership patterns but there were other factors. Scale is of great significance. If one imagines what might have happened if this development had been reserved for the twentieth century, one can see three alternatives, either a series of individual villas, or a mass of small boxes on a grid of streets or big blocks, doing their best to ignore the contours. Only the eighteenth and early nineteenth centuries could have given what we have today: groups of buildings that defer to the hillside whilst

Prince's Buildings: the central pedimented block

Drawing of the original form of Prince's Buildings (top) and Ashley Place, Montpelier (bottom)

Royal York Crescent

enhancing it. From a distance, across the river to the south, the four great structures, Windsor Terrace, the Paragon, Royal York and Cornwallis Crescents fill the hill and at the same time proclaim their genius, because of the perfect clarity of the way the buildings relate to the landscape.

This feeling of perfect balance seems to work close to as well, in spite of the fact that the buildings, on the whole, are quite different in detail from how they would have been intended to look originally. Royal York was originally meant to be a brick crescent and without balconies at the first floor. Cornwallis, too, would have had a brick entrance front. The stucco walls and the wrought-iron balconies were entirely a product of the nineteenth century. Nevertheless, the rules remained the same during the decade or two whilst the buildings remained incomplete so that when the process recommenced it was not left to individual tenants as to whether they preferred brick or stucco: everyone got the same white paint and everyone got a balcony of the same design although individual variations were permitted on the detailed design of the ironwork. There was a certainty about life and shared assumptions that allowed society to operate within closely constrained limits. The detailed description of the form of houses in legal documents was one example of this. The layout of Clifton, the city squares and the grand display of Bath are direct results of this attitude of mind. The early decades of the new century were actually the last moments of this era. Terraces, crescents and squares continued to be built but a greater emphasis on individuality was apparent and single or paired villas appeared. The development of the upper end of Queen's Road before 1850 illustrates this with its Regency-like villas interspersed with terraces and culminating in a great square, whose name heralds the new era.

It is probable that all the designers involved in work at Clifton knew, at least approximately, how the hillside was to be developed but the individual and most important features were devised by individuals and were not subject to an overall control. The enormous bastion on which Windsor Terrace was built and the massive base and pavement that ensures Royal York's dominant position, the sweep of Cornwallis Crescent, and the decision to reverse the curve of the Paragon, between them make Clifton unique, the masterpiece that it is. William Paty can be shown to have contributed only two of these. In fact, Clifton provided an inspiring site that was, luckily, developed by designers who were able to respond inspirationally to it. Even the thirty-year building time did not wreck but improved the original concept so that now, in a post coal-fires era, we can renew the original glories with a lick of paint and a dash of cold water, whenever we want to.

CHRIST CHURCH

In 1789 William would have been concerned particularly with the interior of Christchurch, then building. The essential difference, in design terms, between his father and himself was that he was both aware of and anxious to practise in the style of the London designers. It was twelve years since his student years in London and, at last, Thomas was releasing the reins and had given over control of the new church to William and John. It needs to be said that apart from their registration as students, in 1772 for John and 1775 for William, there is no other evidence about their performance as students nor of the completion of any projects. Thomas Paty was advertising his practice as 'Thomas Paty and Sons' by 1777 when they must have been back in Bristol.

Whatever they achieved as students, they would certainly have been aware of what was going on in London in the 1770s. It has been suggested that St. Martin-in-the-Fields was the main influence upon the boys, yet that building was fifty years old in 1775. This could not have been an up-to-the-minute structure for an eighteen-year old in search of inspiration. William, or William and John perhaps borrowed the Corinthian columns with their individual entablatures from James Gibbs but he/they were looking to men who were building at that minute. The brothers Adam, William Chambers, Sir Robert Taylor, James Wyatt and George Dance the Younger were the men of the moment and whose influence must have been considerable.

The most obvious and most dramatic link was with the last named, George Dance. In the Academy Edition architectural monograph on John Soane, published in 1983, Sir John Summerson demonstrated that Dance was both tutor to and precursor of Soane and he demonstrated that some of Soane's most brilliant work at the Bank of England derived directly from the younger George Dance, and that the first drawings for the Bank Stock Office were made by Dance as a result of discussions between the two men. Summerson stated that George Dance's first work, All Hallows, London Wall, built in 1765 was the first neo-classical building in England and that a later work, the Guildhall Common Council Chamber, built in 1777, 'forestalls much of what we are apt to think of as unique to Soane. The Chamber (demolished in 1906) was a square hall covered by a dome with a central occulus. The dome was of a type which had not been seen before in England and not very frequently elsewhere. Its main characteristic is that instead of rising from separate pendentives as do most Byzantine and Renaissance domes, it is itself a pendentive structure, consisting of one continuous spherical surface ... pendentive dome may be adopted as the appropriate [name for it] ... After Dance's use of the "pendentive dome" at the Guildhall it is not found again until Soane takes it up, first in the Drawing Room at Wimpole Hall (1791–3) and then in the Bank Stock Office of 1792.'

But Christ Church, Bristol intervenes, with a complete series of pendentive domes. It was designed in 1785 or 1786 and the church completed and reconsecrated in 1790. The nave and aisles comprise no fewer than twelve shallow domes, contrived on rectangles rather than square plans, but in spite of the concomitant distortions each is complete with its pendentives integral.

In the four-bay nave a hemi-spherical bite is taken out of the dome on each of the short sides, in order to correct the geometry and allow the pendentives to be more nearly symmetrical and consequently less twisted. The bites actually add to the complexity of form in the ceiling and break down the compartmentalisation of the space so that there is a more flowing quality between the nave and the aisles than might be expected. The bite, whose inspiration could have come from All Hallows Church, London Wall, where George Dance the Younger had taken dramatic bites out of his barrel-vaulted roof to light his massive clerestorey windows, more or less eliminates the boundary effect between the aisles and the nave and the ceiling literally dances across the whole of the space of the church, in a way that has one searching for analogies with ballerinas. It is lucky that this ceiling was not required to be 'fire-proof' as John Soane's Bank ones were.

The overall effect of this marvellous, undulating surface of amazing complexity is unique and is in no way imitative of anyone else's work except insofar as it attempted to pre-empt what John Soane might come up with in the next year or so. It has to be admitted that William Paty and his brother did not get it quite right, partly because of their use of a rectangular grid and partly because of their other metropolitan love for Adamesque decoration, so that no-one has previously spotted the link between this work and that of George Dance and his genius pupil. In fact, John and William drew from the same source as did John Soane and, whilst Soane went on to Italy to nurture his burgeoning genius and build up his contacts with aristocrats, the young Patys returned to their father in Bristol to brood over their experiences and design monuments, until the amazing chance presented itself with the ancient Christ Church, threatening to fall about its parishioners' ears.

It is perhaps necessary to look at the time that John and William Paty spent in London at the Royal Academy. John was registered in 1772, only four years after its foundation, when he was still 17 years old, and William went up in 1775 when he was 18, by which time their father was sixty-two years old. He was clearly determined that the firm should be absolutely professional and second to none. He must have been a man of great determination. John Soane was already a student at the Academy, about a year older than John Paty and by 1772 already a Silver Medallist. In 1776, in the Patys' last year there, he was to win the Gold Medal with his magnificent design for a Triumphal Bridge. He would have been a distant hero figure to the young provincials, who may have had closer contact with George Dance, who was a Visitor (tutor) at the Academy where he had been one of the founding members. He was a warm, sociable and entertaining man of great popularity, whilst his pupil, Soane was a solemn, introspective person who did not mix easily unless with those who could advance his career or help him to advance architecture itself. It might be that William, at least, worked for Dance when he was in London. In this way he could have gained the knowledge about the Guildhall project which was to

Christ Church interior [photo: Gordon Kelsey]

Interior of All Hallows Church, London, George Dance

be built in 1777 and which must be the prime source for the Paty design of Christ Church. It does not seem likely that they could have gained a close enough relationship with his master through the formal and occasional contacts that the Academy classroom would afford. If William had worked with George Dance it could have been that the first contact was made by Thomas who had possibly known George Dance the Elder in 1740 when he was a contender for the Bristol Exchange before John Wood 'emerged'.

All that is hypothetical; what is certain is that the ceiling at Christ Church was at the forefront of neo-classicism and had pendentive domes, used previously only by George Dance the Younger and yet to be used by John Soane and developed by him as part of his unique design language, particularly in the Bank of England. It is even conceivable that the design for Christ Church was William's student project, discussed with George Dance himself.

Commentators have failed to notice the pendentive domes or the historical significance of the ceiling shape at Christ Church. The suggestion that the whole idea came from one of the Transfer Offices at the Bank of England by Sir Robert Taylor is actually tantamount to saying that the idea came from St. Martin-in-the-Fields which is the source that Taylor used at the Bank. The only differences between that church and the bank are that the arcade is returned at the ends, so that the ceiling seems to end in a half dome and the use of small central circular roof-light domes, which were not used in St. Martin's. St Martin-in-the-Fields has previously been held up as the main source for inspiration at Christ Church and of course, the Corinthian columns, each with its own complete entablature, are an obvious source, but above this, William and perhaps John Paty too, devised a delicate, dancing roof form that was, and perhaps still is, unique, and which was the first use in England of a series of pendentive domes.

This remarkably modelled ceiling makes contact with a man who is still greatly undervalued but who deserves to be recognised as the most important innovator in the world of architecture at that time, a worthy successor to Claude-Nicholas Le Doux. The decorative motifs used at Christ Church, however, were under another's influence, which has hidden the significance of the pendentive domes. Robert Adam decoration has been laid on thickly and his design guidance is apparent on the furnishings too. At the Bank of England, John Soane was about to almost eliminate foliage and tendrils and replace them with Greek frets, fans and lines. If William Paty had used Soanean rather than Adamesque motifs on his surfaces, this interior would have been much more easily recognisable as akin to the great lost interiors of the Bank. But this was all in position at least two years before Soane's Bank of England interiors were created. Historically and architecturally, the interior of Christ Church was and is of first rank significance. The Victorian mess-up that has displaced the original east end should be removed and the reredos and furniture set back in position so that the brilliant design can be seen again in its full glory. Apart from the unique vault system of Bristol Cathedral, there is no more significant space in Bristol.

PORTLAND SQUARE

After this time, William Paty found himself both on his own and very busy. It may have been this that ensured that he was not to repeat this design triumph, or it may have been that the genius was in fact John, although the designer of Blaise Castle House demonstrates a similar quality of genius and seems to confirm his status as designer of both. Of the other buildings made in William's last decade, the Great George Street houses illustrate the way that William refined his father's work. They symbolise all that the Patys did best. Simplicity and austerity are their hallmarks, the art of building beautifully is embodied in them and numbers 7, 23 and 25 in particular stand as a joint monument to Thomas and William Paty.

Portland Square is not usually considered as by William Paty, being attributed to Daniel Hague, who actually advertised the project in 1790 in the Bristol newspapers when he offered lots of void ground with sewers laid to them and 'Plans of which, and the elevations, may be seen at Daniel Hague's, architect and builder, in Wilder Street'. The square had a sad and prolonged building history and, like much of Clifton, was not completed until about 1820, but it was of very advanced design and is the only unified Georgian square in the city. There is a character of metropolitan grandeur and a distinct Adamesque flavour that almost demands William Paty's involvement and, as he and Hague were then already working together on the hospital, it is feasible that they were working together here, too. Indeed, Daniel Hague was a jobber and not capable of such sophistication unaided. Portland Square was grand in scale as well as in design quality. The details particularly demand Paty authorship, although they were often new and unusual for Bristol. The basic form of the square is straight-forward with three of the corners having two roads in at right angles but outside the geometry of the square. The fourth has just one road in, the 'missing' road coming in at the centre of the western rank of houses, making a link with the earlier Brunswick Square, which, in Bristol's inelegant (not shipshape) fashion, was never completed and never designed as a whole. This street, called Surrey Street, comes into the Square directly opposite St. Paul's church which is a grandiose and extravagant piece of gothick, again usually attributed to Daniel Hague and perhaps helped along by William Paty. It makes a suitable and dramatic stop to the vista and provides a proper emphasis to the square, although many people feel that it is too *outré* to be acceptable there.

In detail, the buildings are very simple and straightforward in the Bristol fashion. The ground floor is rusticated and does not have the usual lesenes to separate the properties but the doorways are grander than normal, with

Portland Square, north and east sides

Portland Square: a standard three-bay house as an end feature, without fourth-floor emphasis

A central four-bay house with Grecian pilasters and a fourth (attic) floor

Berkeley Square Hotel with Grecian pilasters [Stephen Morris]

three-quarter round columns rather than simple pilasters. Above the standard string course, there are two stories of absolutely plain fenestration and a modillioned cornice and a plain parapet, except at the ends and in the centre of the north and south blocks where a third floor rises to emphasise the pavilions which are set forward as well. The centre pieces are further emphasised with pilasters with Corinthian capitals of Grecian form but of uncertain provenance, but which match those used by William Paty on what is now called the Berkeley Square Hotel.

For a brief time, in the nineteenth century, Portland Square achieved its designer's intentions and was an area of elegance and fashion but it soon descended into an industrial area, the handsome interiors devastated or destroyed. After many years of neglect, the outward character of the great square has been restored but only fragments of the interiors remain. Happily, one house, No. 27 Portland Square, has been well restored internally.

BLAISE CASTLE HOUSE

Blaise Castle House was built for John Scandrett Harford by William Paty in 1796. John Nash added the Conservatory and the Dairy in 1804/6 and built the delightful Blaise Hamlet in 1811. In 1832/3 Charles Cockerell added the Picture Gallery to the house, with the Ionic portico. Paty has actually received little credit for his work, as his name has been overshadowed by those of his more luminous colleagues who made the additions. In fact, this commission was probably the only one where he was free to express his vision of the future of architecture in just the way he had at Christ Church. A monied and intelligent client was ready and anxious to support an advanced design. The main pavilion, with its strong, horizontal-emphasis ground floor rustication, the recessed panels over the first-floor windows, the relieving arches over important windows and the elegant circular entrance portico, very Greek and very advanced, leading many to think that 'he received in his professional exertions, the assistance of Mr. Nash,' as J. Brewer suggested in '*Deliniations of the County of Gloucestershire*' (J. & H.S. Storer, 1824). There is in fact no evidence that Nash was in any way involved then. At the time, Nash was developing his relationship with Humphrey Repton who was preparing his 'Red Book' for Blaise. Repton interfered only to the extent of recommending that the house be raised a little higher out of the ground. The building looks like Bristol buildings of the 1820s or later. It is a quiet, distinguished and very subtle essay in William Paty's favourite Adamesque manner. The essential characteristic, however, is one that I have commented on before, in relation to his father Thomas's work: that is the simplicity and austerity of the design and how it relates to Quaker attitudes.

The three main elevations of the house are complementary and somehow combine magnificence and modest understatement. The entrance front has a

Blaise Castle House

Blaise Castle House staircase

bold, absolutely plain pediment over the amazing entrance porch of a half circle of Ionic columns, which, on approach, is revealed as a complete circle, one half eaten out of the volume of the house, covered by a shallow dome. What at first seemed like a rather plain entrance turns into a major ceremonial introductory place with the entrance doors flanked by a pair of niches that need Greek statuary in them. The ground floor of the house is emphasised by horizontal rustications of rectangular section, now filled with timber battens to prevent vandal climbers. At first floor level, the fenestration is emphasised with an architrave and a simple flat cornice and above are blind panels or, at the centre bays, the frieze of the modillioned cornice. Above, on the entrance front, the plain pediment is flanked by a balustrade, and on the others, the centre is a blind panel that might have been intended for carving. The roof above is taken up steeply in Welsh slate to flat leads and has a strongly modelled chimney stack at each corner.

On the south-east elevation, the almost square form is interrupted by the addition of Charles Cockerell's Ionic portico of the Picture Gallery. It actually breaks down the originally intended cool elegance of an isolated pavilion in its landscape. The portico does not enhance the original, though it does make a link between the house and the conservatory; others have suggested that it was what the house needed to turn it into a proper 'gentleman's residence'.

The house as William Paty left it was in many ways a perfect expression of his genius. He was able to record his intentions for the nineteenth century. For the first time since his work at Christ Church, he could express himself through a client who gave him freedom and complete trust. Together, they are both the earliest and the most advanced neo-classical works in Bristol. The circular Ionic porch at Blaise is its most sophisticated feature and the most hidden. It sums up the quandary of the Quaker banker, seeking grandeur quietly. The marvellous cream-coloured roach-bed Portland stone of the pavement carries over the threshold into the cool and elegant entrance hall. Plaster casts of parts of the Panathenaic Frieze of the Parthenon and large medallions of neo-classic form, together with a cast of Michelangelo's *Lorenzo di Medici* decorate the space, chosen by John S. Harford Junior and set up in the 1820s, but exactly in tune with this very advanced design.

At the back and to the left stands the staircase, one of the finest examples of a so-called cantilever staircase, which is actually fully load-bearing as each of the stone treads sits firmly on the one below it as well as being built into the wall. The cantilever impression is so strong that it fooled the City Engineer in the 1950s into carrying out a complicated and entirely unnecessary steel prop underneath the middle of the first flight, which remains as a monument to municipal anxiety. The staircase has a fine and very delicate wrought-iron balustrade with gilded acanthus leaves and a fine mahogany handrail. The square space at the head of the stairs is roofed with a glass dome that floods the whole interior with light. The side walls are pierced with a pair of arcaded openings on both sides that have been firmly attributed to Charles Cockerell but are in fact entirely William Paty. The far wall beyond the head of the stair has been spanned and is supported with a pair of gigantic plaster consol brackets which may be by Cockerell, but on the whole this beautiful and generous staircase hall is the work of William Paty and his (1796) plasterers. To round out the perfection of the 'public spaces' of the house, the floor here on the first floor up to the entrances to the rooms is built in the same cream Portland stone. This superb and unifying gesture demonstrates an architect who was absolutely sure of himself and of where he was going. That he died at the age of 43 in 1800 was a tragedy for Bristol.

Just as his design for Christ Church was of unique importance, so was this house important. Completed two years before the turn of the century, it was as advanced in neo-classical terms as anything in the country. Robert Adam, who had died four years before the start at Henbury, was never as purely Greek and austere as this, nor were any of his followers who have submerged Paty's name here.

Civic Improvements

Most of the known facts about the Paty family are contained in entries in the files of the Bristol Record Office. It was in the eighteenth century that it became usual for ordinary mortals' lives to be recorded, when their affairs related directly to civic matters. In Bristol, the system where civic activity was controlled by the committee system, was well developed. Some committee minutes recorded the development of building projects and the most important of these was the record of the Committee for Building the Exchange and Markets, whose first meeting was held on June 6th, 1739 and which met weekly for several years, then monthly and then occasionally until April 25th, 1768. There were in all 372 meetings, all of which were recorded, sometimes in great detail, so that the day-to-day working lives of architects, builders and craftsmen are available to us now. The Patys were not the most important members of that group of builders but Thomas is mentioned frequently and James(1) is recorded once or twice.

Thomas first appeared in the Minute Book as working on the Exchange in an entry for May 8th, 1741 which shows that he received £1 for carving the inscription that Mr Recorder had devised for the foundation stone. This was in Latin, and in translation reads:

In the reign of
the Pious Happy and August
GEORGE THE SECOND
Protector of
LIBERTY
and
Merchandise
at Home and Abroad.

Henry Combe, Mayor
laid the first stone of this Aedifice
Built by the Vote of the Citizens
and with the Public Money,
in the year of Christ
MDCCXL.

It was placed at the north-east corner of the building, it weighed two tons and is, presumably, still there, with the lettering covered by a thick sheet of lead and with the building on top of it – a true foundation stone.

Thomas Paty's pay of £1 was actually at a rate of 1$\frac{1}{4}$d per letter which was quite high. He charged $\frac{1}{4}$d a letter on memorial stones. Thereafter his name appeared against payments for carving in July 1742, September 1743, February 1743/4, September 1744, February 1749/50 September 1751, September 1752 and May 1754, and his name is there at the record of the very last meeting, dated April 20th, 1768 where 'the committee, having had several previous meetings and agreed to erect several Market stalls in the Market, near the Post Office, agreeable to the plan, elevation and instructions drawn by Mr. Thomas Patty, the said committee this day agreed with Thomas Killroy and others to have the same executed for the sum of £325 and an order is signed accordingly.'

Both Thomas Paty and James Paty(1) tendered for the Freemason's Contract for the Exchange. Thomas's tender at £2,312.16.0 was the lowest 'Bristolian' tender, there being two 'Bathonian' bids below that price at £2,087.4.6. from John Pitcher and one of £1,967.18.9. from William Biggs, who won the contract. James Paty(1)'s bid was for £2,655.16.8., one of the highest tenders.

Most of the documentation in the Record Office about the Patys concerns property. One, from January 1749/50, is for an agreement to sell a crane, then belonging to Paul Fisher, to Thomas Paty, who bought the lease for £120, whilst Mr. Fisher retained the right to use both the quay and the crane. Paty also agreed to a ground rent charge of £40 per annum. Paul Fisher's mansion on Clifton Hill had just been completed and Mr. Paty's practice and workshop were developing into its busiest period when the flow of Bath stone and foreign marbles would have been high enough to sustain this expenditure. Another document contains a number of drawings for monuments and has a handsomely written letter from Mr Paty setting out his terms for a monument which he can make for £45.10. exclusive of inscription but saying that black marble of the size proposed could take 'some Months' but that if Dove Marble or mixed Rundella marble were substituted, then 'it might be completed in two months or less'.

In item 00971(1) an agreement for building in Great George Street, with the proprietors of Bullocks Park with Lowbridge Bright, dated December 21st, 1784, demonstrated the way that Thomas Paty tied up purchasers, so that they built in the way he intended:

> Agreement between John Daubeney, Merchant and wife and daughter as administrators of John Brown, deceased, Margaretta Tyndall, John Blagdon Hall, Richard Blake – and Lowbridge Bright of the other part. Lowbridge Bright, desirous of building one or more houses and stables on plots marked out and allotted for him by Mr. Thomas Paty architect. All that piece of ground, containing in front to Great George Street one

> hundred and two feet bounded on west by late Mr. Farrell's land and on east by a lane or way 20 feet wide leading to a parallel lane. Ground rent. £28. – Shall within three years lay out and expend the sum of £2,000. at least building one or more good and substantial messuages or dwelling houses on the said ground so to be demised agreeable to the regulations already complied with by the other parties who have built in Great George St. but subject nevertheless to such alterations therefrom as are herein specified and such houses shall be built in a regular and workmanlike manner, leaving an area in front of each house of 5 feet inclosed with iron pallisades.
> To be built in front of freestone or brick ornamented with freestone. Shall not be less than 24 feet in front and shall be built uniform in front to those already built and agreeable to the regulations for building the fronts as contained in the demise of ground there heretofore made to the late Mr. Joseph Farrell. The road to be pitched to the centre of Great George Street.

Mr. Bright was only required to build one house to the value of £2,000 although the agreement allowed him to build a second. The site is identified in an attached plan as the site of 27 and 29 Great George Street. The second document in this record, 00971(2), is an agreement between Mr. Bright and James Morgan where it is stated that Bright declines to build (having already built No. 29 on half the site), sells to Morgan a 61 ft. plot on which he imposes a further requirement to build no deeper than 47 ft (this being the depth of his own neighbouring property). Mr. Bright had built his property in brick, with Bath stone decorations but Mr. Morgan built in Bath stone, matching the houses further down the street.

Item 04226(3)b. records a number of transactions between John Lewis with Thomas Paty and various house and other property owners in the scheme to develop a new street, running from Corn Street to the Quay, to be called Clare Street. It demonstrates that negotiations were sometimes protracted and even involved going to law to force the sale of some properties. When an owner refused to accept an offer made, the law then required the would-be purchaser (in this case, Lewis and Paty) to tell out the offer price, in cash, to the owner, to demonstrate his (their) ability to complete the transaction. When refused, it was necessary to record this to a jury who would then be asked to visit the site to assess whether the proposed price was a fair one and then recommend whether the sale should be forced on the owner. This arrangement was recorded in relation to a property in Marsh Street owned by a Mr. Hartnell, with a number of other properties on the site and in Marsh Street, some even as far away as adjacent to the end of King Street, a long way from the new street. It is possible that someone, perhaps Thoms Paty himself, was taking advantage of the scheme to promote an enhanced redevelopment project.

Negotiations with the Church over the purchase of St. Leonard's and its subsequent demolition are recorded and in this case, Lewis and Paty apparently succeed in improving the Subscribers' profit by 20 guineas. Mr. Paty's payment 'for his trouble etc' of £157.10.0. is recorded, as is the final meeting of the committee when the accounts are checked and Messrs Lewis and Paty pay over the £6,101.16.4. profit on the scheme to the subscribers. Later documents concern Thomas's son William, who was a City Surveyor. An indenture dated

> In the 32nd year of the Reign of George III (1793) between Peter Morris, House Carpenter, Jacob Kirby, James Leman, Gents., Robert Simpson Apoth., John Brittain, China Manuf., for the one part and
> James Lockier Mercht.,
> William Paty, Architect,
> Philip Jones Merchant,
> to sell to the latter, land on the Backfield in Parish of St. Paul (late St. James) 13 ft × 45 ft + buildings on it and another property in Wilder Street (the Sign of the Three Compasses), property on Milk Street/York Street and property (with houses built by George Salter) on Gloucester Street, 30 ft × 80 ft bounded by Norfolk Street capital property by Peter Morris on the Green Close, Portland House 72ft. in front, 110 ft in depth bounded by a new street, Alfred Street. All that part called Green Close together with Meeting House or Chapel and other erections now building and also all on the east side of York Street also west side of Gloucs. Street and Land at Hooks Mile Road leading from Stokes Croft 3+ acres 700′ × 250′ 1+ acre at Wilder Street and Bishop Street. Another piece, bounded by Portland Street (east side, part of Green Close)
> All for one year for a peppercorn.

This and a second indenture between the same parties for properties by the Half Moon Hotel, the Cat and Feather Inn, Prior Hill and Dove Street (Dovecot Lane) again for one year, for a peppercorn were in fact forced sales between bankrupt speculators and builders to William Paty and his peers who were, jointly, acting for the Commissioners in Bankruptcy who would eventually re-sell on behalf of the creditors.

A document dated December 21st, 1792 is a release of property in Limekiln Lane from Lady Mill to William Paty and 'a trustee' of a house 'in Limekiln Lane, a house adjoining and a house behind in Warren's Court and one in Frog Lane and all shops cellars sollars Halls Parlours Chambers Kitchens rooms lofts – whatsoever to the said messuages. Price £560.'

In November 1809 there appears a conveyance of a messuage in College Place by the Trustees of Mr. William Paty, deceased to Mrs. Mary Wilmot. The trustees were Maria Bulkeley, William Paty's daughter and George William Paty, his son, who were selling the family home after their mother's death. This marks the end of the Patys in Bristol.

There are a number of drawings by members of the family in the City Plan Books. In Plan Book A, *item 180* is a plan of a property at the corner of Peter Street with Castle Street, dated 1768 and signed by Thomas Paty and Daniel Millard, a carpenter.

Items 238a/b are proposals for a Market in the Parish of St. Augustine's on a site bounded by Brandon Street, College Street, Limekiln Lane and 'Mr. Wellick's Yard', put forward by Samuel Worral in 1771. An estimate of cost by Thomas Paty totalling £1,131.16.8. appears in *item 240.*

Item 263b is a subpoena for 'William Pattey' amongst other 'esquires' to appear at the Guildhall to give evidence in a case between Matthew Concannon (plaintiff) and Samuel Long, Cooper (defendant) on a plea of trespass.

Items 269, 270 and 272 are drawings of Prince Street houses, 'taken by Mr. Wm.Paty in Jan, 1794', a drawing of the side elevation of a crane, perhaps by Thomas Paty and a drawing of Lawfords Gate in 1750 labelled 'plan at West St., Cheese La. & Bull Paunch La.', which also contains an elevation with a pediment and a Royal Coat of Arms. The drawing has prices listed including 'Mr. Patty's masons work £155.0.0'. *Item 274* contains a more detailed study with two elevations. On the back, 'Temple Gate' is crossed out and amended to 'Lawfords Gate'.

In Plan Book B, *item 6* is a plan of Sir Abraham Elton's house in St. James Barton together with a plan entitled 'the Two Large Rooms at the Merchant's Hall' which is a careful drawing in sepia wash, perhaps by Thomas Paty.

Items 17 and 18 are designs (elevation and plan) for a Gothick porch to the Mayor's Chapel, made by Thomas Paty which was built and survived only until 1822 when the whole of the west front was taken down and rebuilt.

Item 82 contains a survey plan of the top of St. Michael's Hill, showing Paul and Clarence Streets and the junctions with Cotham Hill and Hampton Road, which also locates the site of the Gallows. This is a meticulously drawn plan by William Paty which suggests that he was concerned with the development of this northern end of Kingsdown and was probably the author of the delightful 'upside down' group of late Georgian cottages in Trelawney Road.

Item 88 is another fine William Paty plan, dated March 1799, of Lewins Mead and Johnny Ball's Lane, showing the Meeting House of the Unitarians with its semi-circular porch drawn on and then rubbed out, although it was built like that. The porch was a William Paty design and it is probable that he was in charge of the building to Mr William Blackburn's design. *Item 87a* 'taken by Mr Wm. Paty' was a plan of the void ground on Stoney Hill dated March 26th, 1795 which has a drawing of 'Whitchurch's Cranes' drawn on the back of it. *Item 90* is a survey by William Paty of Park Row Avenue and *91* is dated March 2nd, 1791 'taken by Mr. Paty' of Queen's Parade, Brandon Hill, showing it as a terrace of twelve houses and stating that No.s 1–5 were then 'still building'. The plan lists the owners and tenants and notes 'the encroachments' which were the cellars under the pavements in front of the houses. This group of buildings was a late 'opportunistic' development, squeezed on to a site between the Paty workshops and the public domain of Brandon Hill.

Item 94a and b are William Paty plans of Castle Mills Broadware (sic), and Samuel Thomas's premises at Jacob's Well, dated June 25th, 1794.

Item 98a is a Paty plan of 'five tenements intended to be built on St Michael's Hill etc., opposite Mr. Colston's Almshouse'. The house plans are shown in detail. A note states 'The houses were not built to this plan' and the site is still occupied by seventeenth-century jettied houses. Houses above this site in Tankard's Close and on the Hill were a Paty development although, as usual, at another's risk, which is demonstrated by *item 98b* drawn in February 1800 by William Paty of this area and marked 'the property of the assignees of John Mallard (a bankrupt) and others'.

Items 99, 102/3, 104, 105, 110a and 111a all contain William Paty drawings, mostly plans and maps of properties in Queen Square, Castle Street, Little King Street, Old Market Street, Stoney Hill and St. John's Gate, probably mostly to do with his role as a City Surveyor, but some could be of more direct personal significance. *No 117* is a survey drawing of College Green, Frog Lane, College Place, College Street, showing 'Mr. Paty's Yard'.

Item 124 a, b & c is an estimate with elevation and plan, dated April 2nd, 1794 drawn in ink and priced £50.11.6. signed William Paty.

Item 124d is a plan of Bristol Bridge, St. Nicholas Church and 'Site of New Market on the Backs', and *No. 134* is a plan of Portland Square.

Plan Book E contains a Specification and a drawing for a new bridge over the Frome from Broadmead to Duck Lane with estimates from builders 'to make it in accordance with Mr. William Paty's instructions'. Paty described himself here as 'surveyor' but puts in a price himself, two months before the builders' prices.

These last entries, in particular, demonstrate just how active William Paty was, in the last decade of his life, in the pursuit of 'civic improvement' jobs whilst at the same time keeping his workshop, monumental masonry work and his mainstream projects running too.

The Paty Legacy

To assess the significance of the Paty family in Bristol's eighteenth-century architecture, one has to attempt an evaluation of individual contributions and make comparisons between them and other craftsmen/designers of their time.

Problems arise immediately. The first James has not left enough information. We know that he designed and carved about a dozen monuments, the Christ Church Quarter Jacks are said to be his, and he is recorded as having carved one of the Corinthian capitals for the Exchange (for £2.12.6d.). We know that he was master mason on the King Street Library and that he was probably its designer, was perhaps the designer of No. 32 College Green, and it has been suggested that he also designed No. 30 College Green and the rank of houses at the top of Unity Street. I have come to believe that he designed Earnshill in Somerset. We know that he did the stone carving and perhaps the wood carving and joinery at Redland Court. We know that he quoted for the freemasonry contract for the Exchange and that his estimate was the second highest of the five tendered, and this was thought to be because he was then very busy. The evidence, however, is thin and tentative. One cannot, therefore, establish much about his merits, although if all that is possibly by him was actually his, then he could be claimed a significant figure.

In the case of the second James, Thomas's brother, even less information is available. No building designed and built by him, on his own, is known; and the number of monuments thought to be by him is painfully small. He was, however, his brother's partner in some civic improvements projects, so he can be said to have shared in the creation of Park Street and all the other new developments they promoted before his death in 1779, but he remains an enigmatic figure.

With Thomas, the doubts vanish. As a young man, he served masters, the elder John Wood and Isaac Ware at the Exchange and Clifton Hill House and worked on his own account at Redland Chapel. In the 1750s with the Royal Fort, Arno's Court, St. Nicholas Church, St. Michael's Church and the Theatre Royal, projects in Somerset and Gloucestershire, as well as the City Improvement Schemes, he was able to expand his workshop to an extent that gave him virtual control of Bristol's building industry.

By that time, Thomas Paty was combining the roles of building craftsman with those of land agent, surveyor, town planner and architect. He negotiated the purchase of land and property on behalf of the Corporation and mercantile or social groups, replanned areas and designed elevations for new streets, organised contractors and craftsmen and, presumably, arranged for them to buy all they would need from his workshops in due course. Here, he was making staircases, doors, windows, fireplaces, as well as all the Bath Stone details that they would need. His neighbours in Limekiln Lane, plasterers and iron workers, were almost certainly under his supervision or in partnership with him, which meant that he was in control of practically every aspect of any gentleman's domestic building needs. Sometimes, he would build houses himself, but he was more often content to let others build, controlling the design by clauses in the conveyances, and the detail through the products of his workshops. At the same time, he was turning out memorial tablets and larger monuments of a quality that varied between good and brilliant.

A document in the Bristol Record Office, a lawyer's account book for a private subscription venture for the making of Clare Street, throws interesting light on Paty's work. The first entry was for April 26th, 1770. The subscribers formed a company to promote the purchase and redevelopment of an ancient and probably very decrepit area between the end of Corn Street and the quayside. This involved the removal of St. Leonard's Church and the remains of the city wall on which it stood. Although the project was a private one, the Corporation were involved and were keen participants. They (the Mayor and Corporation) appointed Thomas Paty and Mr. John Lewis to act as their agents in buying back the leases of the many properties that they owned, just as Mr Hooke had acted in buying back properties on the site of the Exchange in 1739 and 1740.

On July 3rd, 1776 an agreement between the Subscribers (1), the Mayor and Corporation (2), and John Lewis and Thomas Paty (3) ordered the third party (Lewis and Paty) to pay £6,101.16.4d. 'being the balance outstanding', which was paid on the same day, and which was then agreed to be paid out to subscribers. This enormous sum must have been the profit on the venture, after the buying up, demolitions, rebuilding and reselling had been completed, but would presumably have included the originally deposited subscription monies. Mr. Lewis was an employee of the Corporation and would have been paid a salary. Mr. Paty had been 'paid for his trouble etc.' £157.10.0d. on March 25th, 1775. The subscribers would have been happy with their profit, the Mayor and Corporation would have been happy with a brand new street of smart properties that were highly rated, Mr Paty would have made a deal more than his fee and Mr. Lewis would doubtless have been well looked after. It might be that the (unmentioned) fourth party, the original tenants and leaseholders did not do so well. There is no record of the negotiations between Messrs Paty, Lewis and them, not all of whom were 'poor widows' but they would have been 'standing in the way of progress' if they had stood too much upon their rights in attempting to resist the modernisation of their ancient city.

In a similar manner, Thomas Paty, sometimes with Mr. Lewis and with his brother, too, carried out clearance and rebuilding of large chunks of the old city. At the bridgehead at St. Nicholas, he controlled a massive development, which included Bridge Street, St. Peter Street and Union Street, redefining the south and east sides of the medieval city. Bath Street, on the south side of the river, provided the start for the redevelopment of Redcliffe and on the north over the River Frome, Denmark Street, the Butts and St. Augustine's Parade, which meant that he was involved almost all around the old city. Further to the north-west he was promoting the most important of all the developments, the route into Clifton via Park Street.

The essential thing about the housing developments of these years, controlled by Thomas Paty, his workshops and his designated suppliers, was standardisation, both in overall design and in detail. Park Street demonstrates this. It was meant to put the classic stamp on eighteenth-century Bristol in the same way that John Wood had done in Bath. He used Bath stone more often than he used brick but he was equally skilled in both, using brick not only for tidy rear elevations, but occasionally to provide a special highlight, as he did with the entrance pavilions to Great George Street.

Since the 1920s the top of Park Street has been dominated by the great tower of the University, which, whatever else it may be, is not sensitive to the subtleties of Georgian architecture. Originally, the Royal Fort estate would have formed the barrier there and presented a view to the house, then shining new, whilst one was deflected westward, where the back of Berkeley Square stood, high and dominating, in brick and stone. This still exists but is mostly hidden behind the shops built on their back gardens. This was meant to provide release and change from the regime of Bath stone and as a first intimation of the new, more romantic world of brick-clad Clifton, further hinted at in the delicate curve of Berkeley Crescent ahead. That crescent was not commenced until 1791, so the decision to use brick there must have been William's and not Thomas's. I am sure that both men thought alike on most matters architectural, and brick was used by both when it suited: to ring a change, to provide a contrast or to emphasise domesticity. It was used expressively and compositionally, and the idea that brick denoted poor old Thomas and Bath stone, bright young William, cannot be sustained.

Much of Thomas's work in Clifton was brick. Perhaps the most significant was Albemarle Row, a development of lodging houses in Hotwells, and, less well known, but in fact more important, the triangular layout at Hope Square and Granby Hill, now mutilated, which was built by William but to the design of his by then late father. Further into Clifton, there were also the two brick, Gibbsian-detailed blocks of Prospect House and Boyce's Buildings: built in the 1760s, setting the scene that Thomas Paty envisaged and which William attempted to carry through. Both Royal York Crescent and the entrance front of Cornwallis Crescent were originally built in brick. In the last few years, a house in Royal York Crescent was stripped of its render, in the course of restoration, revealing a hidden glory of very beautiful brickwork.

The output of the workshop, or workshops rather, as everything suggests that the extended family worked mainly through the several workshops in a loose partnership, allowed Thomas to control the domestic building output of the whole city. A list of the projects built from the 1750s to the 1780s demonstrates how the pressures must have built up in the workshops. King Square and Park Street were starting in the 1750s, Albemarle Row, Dowry Parade, Boyce's Buildings, Prospect House, Brunswick Square and Redcliffe Parade were all 1760s work, perhaps not all designed by the Patys, but all composed around Paty-designed details. Bridge Street, Clare Street, College Street, Denmark Street, the Quays and Union Street all date from the following decade, and in the 1780s Charlotte Street, Berkeley Square, the Mall, St. Vincent's Parade, Bellevue and Bath Street emerged out of medieval rubble or virgin ground.

In the 1790s, William Paty was in charge: fresh from his first job, free from his father's influence at Christ Church, where he established his reputation, both in the family and in Bristol generally, and perhaps made a claim to genius. It seemed then that the following decade would be even more fruitful but by 1793 disaster had struck and the Bristol building industry lay in ruins. Royal York and Cornwallis Crescents had been started, Prince's Buildings (the Prince of Wales Crescent) and Sion Hill had been completed or nearly so, Portland Square on the other side of the city, had been laid out and the Paragon was ready to begin. The character and quality of Clifton was established when the war in Europe began in earnest and bankruptcy brought almost every building scheme in Bristol to a halt. Not one of the Clifton projects was finished for years to come, and hardly any of the builders of Royal York or Cornwallis Crescents escaped.

William Paty, however, survived. As with his father before him, he avoided laying out capital on building, but made his money by negotiating land sales and leases, providing designs and stone-work carved to detail, joinery and plaster work and other details, as and when they were needed. Presumably, he would demand payment for material supplied on a monthly basis, as building trade suppliers always have, so his risk would have been kept to a minimum. He was known and trusted by the merchants and by the civic authorities, (he was one of the City's surveyors) as well as by most of the contractors and tradesmen, and he was used to buy up unfinished buildings from bankrupts on behalf of the Commissioners in Bankruptcy and, sometimes, on his own behalf. There is no evidence that he was ever financially embarrassed. His will, proved in January 1801, well before the end of the period of financial crisis, left £1,500 – a great deal of money – to his son George William, before he received his share of the estate, which the executors were asked to convert to stocks and shares to provide regular income as and when necessary. Much of his fortune was in real estate and an abstract from the will shows that in 1809, little if any of the suggested selling of property had taken place, that the widow, Sarah Paty and one of the executors, Thomas King of Bath (his brother-in-law), were dead and that his daughter Maria was widowed and without children.

The period of William's independent practice lasted from 1789 to 1800. He was 43 years old at his death. In spite of the collapse in building, he achieved a lot in a short time, from the marvellous interior of Christ Church to the subtle and sensitive house at Blaise. His contribution to the city's domestic building came mostly in the first part of the decade, before the collapse and so was likely to have been under his father's influence. Certainly, all that he did in Park Street, Charlotte Street, Berkeley Square and Great George Street must be shared and is probably rather more Thomas than William. Hardly any of the Clifton schemes were completed in his life time and most of them were eventually completed quite differently from the original intention. He seems to have been involved in several country houses in Wales and may have been exporting architectural elements to the Americas as well.

The monumental side of his business remained very active; William Paty memorials appeared everywhere and he must have had a quantity-production system operating. It seems unlikely that he, or his father during his maturity, had much time to spare to do anything other than to interfere in the processes of creation of a work of sculpture. The work was always of sound quality but nothing stands out as specially significant. This would be partly because ostentatious tombs were then not fashionable, but the fact is that William Paty left us no genuinely notable sculptural legacy as his father and his uncles had. His father had pre-ordained this, of course, by training John as a sculptor and William as architect; the age of specialisation was already beginning. William shone in the realm to which he was trained.

Two Johns and the third James remain to be discussed. The first John was the son of Thomas's brother James. He took over his father's workshop in 1779 after James's death, and announced himself as ready to draw plans and carry out surveying as well as the more usual stone carving jobs. No monuments or buildings by him have been identified, and there is no information about his relationship with Thomas's firm, but no reason either to assume that he did not continue in the same way as his father had, to work as a part of the Paty partnership.

The second John is a complete mystery. He worked with his father before going to the Royal Academy in 1772 and returned to live with his father in Limekiln Lane afterwards, whilst William was recorded as living in Lamb Street at the age of 17 before he went to London in 1775. It seems that John was the favoured son as well as the eldest, but in the last year of both their lives, John was separate and perhaps out of favour, newly married and living in Bath, with one child, a daughter, unrecognised by her grandfather and, apparently, with another child on the way. I have no doubt that some of the drawings in the Copybook are by John but the problem of identifying drawings, with three draughtsmen contenders, rather than the two that I have said were difficult if not impossible to tell apart, becomes more nearly impossible. Architecturally, John can only have been involved during the last twelve years of Thomas's life. It is possible that as the brothers took over control from the old man of the rebuilding of Christ Church, it was he and not William who masterminded the creation of the brilliant interior but there is no evidence for that and as William was the trained architect and John the sculptor, it seems unlikely.

The third James probably took over his late father's workshop from his mother, who had run it for twenty-five years since James(1)'s death. He took over in 1768 when he became a free burgess and ran it until his death in 1807. He was not married, and I have seen no will. He was a good draughtsman and a fine sculptor, a worthy follower of his father.

Only Thomas and William Paty have left enough evidence for firm assessment, whilst the first and second James provide hints of an architectural presence and the third James and two Johns remain ghostly figures. Nevertheless, they help to define the dynasty and add weight as part of a team. In modern terms, Bristol was then a tiny city. The first census was not taken until 1801 when the population was less than 41,000 or, counting the suburbs, 63,000. In this context there can be no doubt that the Patys made a major, if not *the* major, contribution to the architectural and sculptural life of the city. A map of the buildings designed by, built by or detailed by Patys would demonstrate that their contribution was much greater than that of any other individual, and that remarkable, unrivalled standards were achieved.

Contemporaries

Of contemporary builders/architects of the Patys about five are worth attention, if one excludes the important metropolitan and Bath visitors, whose works provides a defining standard against which judgements can be made. John Wood and Isaac Ware were important and inspirational to Thomas Paty, whose work would have been different, although not necessarily better, if he had not worked under them. Redland Chapel was as good a building as any of his later works, although it lacked the discipline of Palladianism. Without their influence, Paty might have taken off up the blind alley of the baroque. Sir John Vanbrugh's influence was marginal. King's Weston House was hardly in Bristol, and the semi-circular window in the pediment of Redland Chapel and the colonnaded chimney-stacks at Bishopsworth Manor, together with the giant keystones in the local cottages at King's Weston, were the only influence.

Of the several locals, John Strahan's name resonates most strongly. He proved a real threat to John Wood the Elder in Bath, at the start of his career there, as is demonstrated by Wood's animosity to the rather mysterious Scotsman. John Wood made some disastrous mistakes in his first Bath job for his London patron, the Duke of Chandos, where, in building a block of rooming houses (now Chandos Court) he constructed new-fangled water closets, of which the Duke was a great promoter, that failed so miserably that the whole, expensive system had to be sealed off. Chandos declared that he would never employ Wood again as an architect and was set to use Strahan in his place. In the event, this did not happen, although Wood had to suffer the indignity of Strahan's being appointed as his supervisor for his next job. John Wood's description of Strahan as a 'piratical' architect may seem to be rather modest in the circumstances but there is perhaps some truth in it. There is at least a suggestion in my mind that he used other people's skills in the furtherance of his own career.

In Bristol, Strahan's name is firmly associated with the design of Redland Court, although the well known drawing of the south front, as originally intended and now in the British Library, was made by John Jacob de Wilstar, one of the city's surveyors. Thomas Paty has been credited with making the alteration that extended the five bays to seven, but it was James(1) of the Patys who was involved here, between 1732 and 1735, and though there is absolutely no evidence of his involvement other than as a mason-carver, this modest craftsman might well have guided his master's hand. Several houses in the city from the 1720s, including No.s 66, 68 and 70 Prince Street, and

No. 59 Queen Charlotte Street, are said to be by Strahan too. The Prince Street houses are much admired whilst the other is not. It is more or less identical in its details to Rosebury House in Kingsmead Square in Bath, which is firmly attributed to Strahan and is criticised as a coarse and semi-literate piece of baroque. It is very difficult to imagine these two houses as being designed by the same hand as that seen at Redland Court and 66–68 Prince Street. The corpus of works attributed to John Strahan in Bristol and Bath shows such a range, stylistically and in quality, that it could be that he used several different draughtsmen as 'helpers' during his time in Bristol. Strahan would not have been the last architect who needed the support of others to reinforce his business and social skills.

William Halfpenny was a clamorous member of the architectural community in Bristol. Unlike John Strahan, he was always making drawings and signing them, too, so that there was no doubt who made them. He probably built the Coopers' Hall and the Prince Street Assembly Rooms, but he was best known for his attempts to win the contract for the Exchange for which he made at least five separate designs, which he submitted to the Corporation although they claimed never to have commissioned them. He was paid a ludicrous five guineas for them in 1740, and, a year later, after he had written a pathetic, cringeing letter in which he 'humbly hoped that they would pay me what they think proper' and stating that there were 'sixteen drawings, most of them on large folio sheets, which I was nere 5 months completing'. He was a timid and over humble man and the Corporation treated him with contempt; they paid him another five guineas 'in full' for his pains. He was an author of architectural pattern books, which he published with his brother from 1722 until his death in 1755. To Bristolians, however, he was an 'incomer carpenter' who should not be encouraged. All his books, ranging from *Magnum in Parvo, or the Marrow of Architecture* dated 1722 to *Rural Architecture in the Chinese Taste* published in a third edition in the year of his death, are now exceedingly rare and valuable, but were then used by tradesmen masons and carpenters to help them leap the fence into the new profession of architecture. His most important book as far as Bristol was concerned was *Perspective Made Easy*, probably first published in 1728 when he first came to Bristol, which contained a number of views of Bristol scenes, including a view of the Hotwells which was copied onto the famous delftware plate in Bristol Museum and Art Gallery. The book also contained his first design for the Exchange. His books do not seem to have aided his career architecturally or financially. H.M. Colvin recorded that in spite of his twenty titles, he died in debt.

Samuel Glascodine was an active and vigorous man, one of the tradesmen 'translated', who kept his overalls at hand if not on throughout his life. He was the carpenter on the Exchange and architect for the Markets and carpenter again for Clifton Hill House in 1746. He died as a well-to-do burgher, in a comfortable and rather grand house of his own design in Stokes Croft, in 1760. He was variable as an architect. He produced the first of the pavilions to the Exchange which was both respectable and respectful, then, soon after, the much less satisfactory entrance gateway to the Markets in High Street.

James Bridges' role in Bristol's architectural scene and his relationship with Thomas Paty is difficult to understand. All the evidence shows that he was Mr. Tyndall's architect for the Royal Fort and that he produced the plans and elevations which are handsome and honest but which lack unity. A perceived need to demonstrate the quality of his detailing seems to have seduced him into using too much of the available architectural language on what was quite a small house. In consequence, there is a restless and uncomfortable feel that has led some to suggest that the three sides were designed by different individuals, vying with each other, as a way of explaining away the clashes that occur.

Inside the house, Thomas Paty was in charge and the quality of the interior decoration has already been assessed, but much of the outside seems on the face of it to be his also. Indeed, the south front is often attributed to him, with its great three-storey bay window, flanked by masses of Bath stone ashlar, broken pediment doors and delicate Venetian windows above them. In spite of the restraint, though, something is wrong. The Venetian windows are oddly, uncomfortably too small, and three different keystone systems within a narrow compass are disturbing as is the way that the rustication of the bay sets off to enclose the whole of the ground floor but is stopped arbitrarily at an otherwise meaningless change of plane.

On the west front the oddness of the previous detail is accented because the rustication here, contained now properly by the three-bay pediment as a central pavilion, is of a different size. Here, the three central arch-headed windows have a projecting springing course so that the depth of the rustications has to be reduced to accommodate its depth. If the two lines of rustick stonework were projected to the corner of the building, they would not coincide. This smaller rustication does work when considered in the context of the west front, on its own, for it is a neat and carefully detailed Palladian statement when viewed from the centre. Its upper windows are decorated at the first floor with eared architraves and flat and triangular pediments, and at the second floor with eared architraves around the windows of the three central bays and with plain architraves at the outer ones.

The scale and character changes again on the north front where suavity and gaiety are replaced by a stern, even sombre, entrance front. There is little extraneous decoration here: a solemn doorway with Ionic order and, at first floor, three arched windows in the centre, and at second floor, keystones over the middle ones, all very restrained compared to the other elevations, although over-decorated when compared to the grand simplicity of the mansions in Great George Street.

Viewed from the corners, Royal Fort is revealed as a thoroughly mismanaged Palladian exercise with the string and cill course, intended as a unifier, actually providing a means of pointing up the failures. Palladio himself had made life easy for himself just two hundred years earlier, when he built the perfect Villa Capra on a hilltop not unlike the situation here. It was perhaps not possible for Bridges to have selected the same simple solution of matching, balanced facades but if his elevations had been designed with one or perhaps two themes to be restated on each front then the corners could have become links and not barriers as they are and he could have made a house that was truly worthy of its interior. If Thomas Paty had been in charge here, he would have done it better and not felt a need to use the project as an advertisement for his workshop's versatility which is what he actually did.

The last of the Patys' contemporaries to need consideration is Daniel Hague. He worked with both Thomas and William. The new hospital, built by Hague, was designed by Thomas Paty and Sons. I believe that William Paty was the neo-classical designer of Portland Square and it is at least possible that he was the Gothick designer for St. Paul's Church there as well. Internally, it is strongly similar to St. Michael-on-the-Mount-Without, with longer, but very similar, giant columns and strange, double-tier capitals that seem to be cross-bred Tuscan and a new form of Corinthian at St. Paul's and an elaborated Tuscan at the earlier church, whose barrel vault is actually a post-war fancy which replaced the original cove and flat of the Paty ceiling. With the ceiling shape corrected, the similarity between the two spaces becomes startling. The fact that St. Michael's was a Thomas Paty work of 1775–77 suggests that William might have been involved with his father on this intentionally cheap and simple design before and perhaps during his Royal Academy year.

St. Paul's is more interesting externally than has been recognised in the past. Its siting and its presence are bold and very dramatic. Its rather gauche detailing adds to, rather than detracts from, the light and airy character of the composition, which may be the result of the combined efforts of Paty, too busy elsewhere to spend much time on it, the Vicar, keenly interested in the design, and Hague, mostly interested in getting the job done. It looks like a building conceived by a master and carried out by lesser mortals.

Conclusion

To summarize, there can be no doubting the Patys' immense impact on Bristol's eighteenth-century architecture. Thomas, on his own, dominated the Bristol building industry for forty years and his son was preparing to do the same. William's early death deprived him of the chance to make an important contribution to the architecture of the first decades of the new century. The first James had established the family's architectural qualities and William, in too short a life, demonstrated how much they had achieved, but it was Thomas Paty who made the greatest contribution. Although we have no single word of his, except for his will, no portrait or drawing of him and only a newspaper obituary as character reference, we know that he built a massive amount of Bristol. At his best, he was a brilliant architect; he was particularly good as an interior decorator, but we also know that he was sometimes slipshod; he was not a genius or a great master. At the beginning of his career at Redland Chapel, he could not resolve the problems he set himself in the east and west ends of the interior; at Ston Easton in Somerset, he was not able to push Mr. Hippsley Coxe into anything other than a a rather gloomy make-over of the previous structure externally, whilst achieving some marvellous interior spaces, and the dreadful mess of Beacon House in Painswick, again masking a brilliant interior, all suggest a man who was not good enough to override the problems posed by anxious and over-cautious clients. In some ways one could say he was a small-time man for a small-time city, but then again he was more than this.

With three craft workshops and an extended family, a determined business ability plus a fairly basic architectural capacity, allied to his own sculptural and wood carving skills, Thomas Paty forged Bristol's architectural form from 1750 until not his own death, but his son William's, in 1800. There is a strange, almost mystic relationship between the two, best seen in Great George Street and Charlotte Street, where William built the most perfect of Thomas's works. I have a greater personal attachment to No.25, but No.7 Great George Street is, truly, the building that marks Thoms Paty's supreme achievement and, at the same time, summarises what the Paty family did for Bristol.

Thomas and William Paty created a Bristol style that fitted Bristol merchants, that required simplicity and good proportions and 'honest to God' straightforwardness. The influences were entirely Andrea Palladio as seen by Isaac Ware in Thomas; then, touched by Robert Adam, George Dance and John Soane, in William.

The Paty Copybook

The collection of 138 drawings was in the RWA School of Architecture Library which passed to the University of Bristol Library in 1963. Ten of the items are drawings of fireplaces, two are of buildings or building projects, one is an etching and the remaining 125 are drawings for funerary monuments. Almost all the drawings are eighteenth-century in date with just 18 or 19 from the nineteenth century, although only three drawings are actually dated. These are the drawings which have details of the lettering that was intended for them.

Traditionally, the collection has been called 'the Paty Copybook' and most of the drawings seem to have been made by one or other of the Patys but other draughtsmen have contributed. Only one drawing is signed by a Paty – William, and it is an unremarkable example (No.25). Thomas certainly contributed and it may be that he contributed most. Certainly Thomas and William between them made the majority. As for the other members of the family, things are not so easy. On their own, the drawings could not be identified but a number of monuments that are signed relate to drawings that can be identified as by one or other of them.

The Paty Copybook entered the School of Architecture Library in 1930 via the late Eustace Button, then Secretary to the School Council and Tutor in the History of Architecture. He had just purchased the practice of a firm once called Foster, Wood and Awdry and the volume had been part of their archive. The original James Foster had been William Paty's apprentice and assistant who set up an architectural practice after William's death. The firm, under various titles, survived through the whole of the nineteenth century and most of the last.

The Copybook itself is not so easy to date because it is a compilation, assembled over a long period. The earliest drawing in the book seems to be the one that links with a monument in Evercreech Church in Somerset which is dated 1715, whilst the last drawing appears to be one on Whatman detail paper which has a watermark date of 1833. In fact, this drawing is an isolated item and the last actual drawing for a monument is one by Henry Wood which matches a monument in Bristol Cathedral dated 1815. This gives a safe one hundred years for the Paty Copybook of 1715–1815.

The binding of the book is of no help. When I first saw it in 1960 or thereabouts, it was in a disbound state without back or covers and it was decided to lift the drawings from the flimsy dark red pages of its original 'album' or 'scrapbook' and remount them onto cartridge paper, imperial size, folded once. It was also decided to reassemble them in a more convenient manner so that the drawings would be subdivided into categories, separating the architectural from the funerary and subdividing the monuments into four types. This was all done, without recording the original sequence of the drawings and it was done innocently in the hope that it would make the collection more accessible.

Regrettable as that may be, the sorting of the drawings is now as follows:

1. Monuments with a funeral urn. (86)
2. Monuments with figures or portraits. (8)
3. Monuments with heraldic badges or other decorative elements. (29)
4. Architectural. (2 architectural drawings, one print of Nelson's memorial in Hereford and 10 drawings for fireplaces)

There have been a number of references to the Copybook in previous publications. These include *The Eighteenth Century Architecture of Bristol* by C.F.W. Dening in which two of the drawings are illustrated, *The Georgian Buildings of Bristol* by Walter Ison, which records its entry into the School of Architecture, and my *Catalogue of the School Library* of 1963. H.M. Colvin in his *Biographical Dictionary of English Architects, 1660–1840* refers to it as 'extant according to Dening'.

The Copybook was presumably intended as a proper catalogue from which grieving widows could select the most desirable and fitting memorial for their loved one, although they were sometimes selected from stock in the yard. There is one memorial to a 16-year old girl in Bristol Cathedral which is signed 'W. Paty' although the date of the girl's death was four years after his own.

Examples of monuments can be found in churches all over the West Country, in Wales and even some in the north. Exports were made to Barbados, the West Indies and the USA.

The stylistic differences between Thomas and William Paty are obscure because it is never clear how much father and son interacted. All that can be said for sure is that Thomas's work until 1777 was likely to be free of the influence of his sons and it is not until after 1789, at Thomas's death, that William was free from his father's influence.

It may be possible, on the other hand, to trace characteristics that are typical of Thomas or William that allow one to be specific, although the waters are 'muddied' by the possible intervention of designers whose qualities are unknown, like Thomas's brother James and William's brother John.

Tim Mowl has identified a tendency towards Gibbsian detail in Thomas and a tendency to gothicising with James(2), but the only firm change is the clear emergence of neo-classicism in William's most important works at Christ Church and Blaise Castle. As far as the collection of drawings is concerned, style is often a better marker than drawing technique particularly for Thomas and William who are scarcely possible to tell apart as draughtsmen. Only a very few drawings have been signed or inscribed and they have been jumbled chronologically and they were added to by Mr. Henry Wood, who bought the workshop in 1801. Although his drawings are fairly easily recognisable it seems that he also at times added his signature to William or even Thomas Paty drawings. In the end, one can only select out the drawings with cherubs or cherubs' heads as being by Thomas and ones with standing females in Grecian robes, leaning on urns, as William's.

There is one other factor about the drawings that has not been mentioned previously: the collection came into the hands of Henry Wood after his takeover but it ended up in Foster, Wood and Awdry's archive. Henry Wood was not the Wood of the firm; he was a young architect who joined in partnership with the original James Foster's grandson in 1847. It is possible that he was a son or grandson of Henry Wood but I have no information on this. Such a relationship would allow the transfer of the drawings between the two organisations, which were, otherwise, entirely separate. This is probably what happened.

The catalogue is organised as follows:

Type of paper used. Watermarks if any. Date, if any.
Size in millimetres. Width first.
Materials used (pencil, ink, wash etc).
Description.
Any inscriptions.
Location of any known comparable monument.
Designer attribution.

The Catalogue

MONUMENTS WITH A FUNERAL URN

1

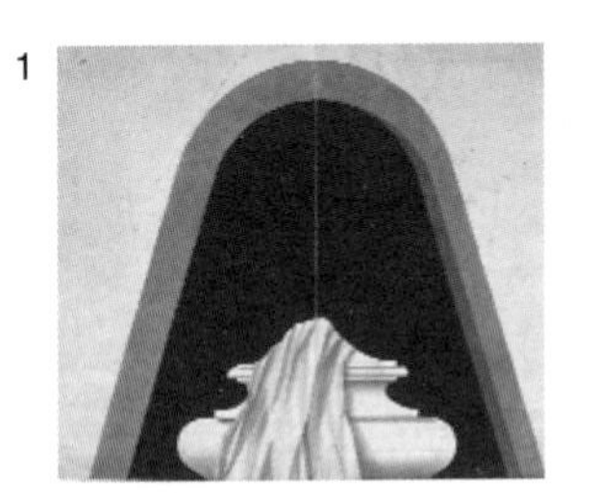

1. Front cover. Cartridge. 31.5 × 22.5.
Black ink and wash. A fragment. The upper part of a pyramidal monument with a semi-circular top. Black with grey edging. The top of an urn and cover in white with a mourning cloth over it. A fine neo-classical design.
Inscribed. 5/- 3.
IX 40.
This would have been an important design. None identified.

Henry Wood

1a

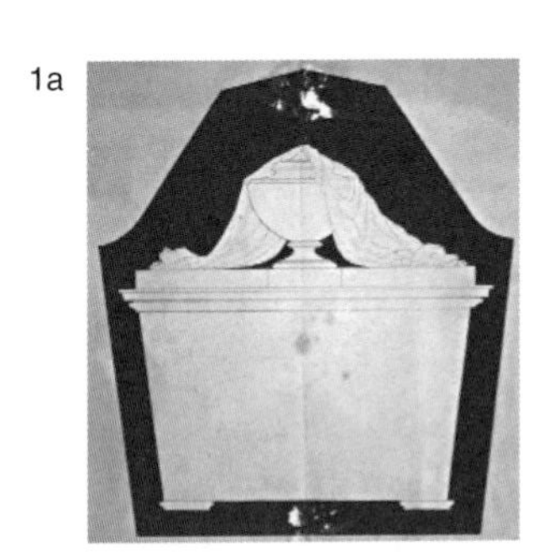

1a. Verso. Cartridge. 31.5 × 22.5.
Black ink with black ink wash. A black slab with battered sides and a quadrangular top forming a squat pyramidal shape containing a memorial slab in the form of a chest or coffer with battered sides and a flat top with a neo-classical cornice. On this a squat urn and cover, draped with a mourning cloth. Carefully drawn in outline on the black ink background. Urn is similar to the one above but draped differently.
Inscribed. No. 1.
4.0.
3.9. IX
Both this and the above are drawn to larger than usual scale and may have been working details at half full size. See also Nos 22 and 27.

Henry Wood

2

2. Cream wove paper. 13.5 × 23.5 cut to shape of monument.
Brown ink and grey wash. A plain panel with semi-circular base on a dark background with pilaster strips supporting caps with rosettes which support a classical cornice which, in turn, supports a reeded pot with foliate handles on a shaped top which is completed with a conical lid. The top is a pyramidal panel with a semi-circular shaped head on a shouldered, curved lower section of dark-coloured stone with a lighter border. The base of the memorial has a plain shield with supporters in the form of crossed quills.

Inscribed; Wood, Bristol, but possibly William or John Paty, as Thomas Paty and Sons. Sepia ink.

3

3. Wove paper 146 × 204.
Grey ink, grey wash watercolours. White marble on blue-grey veined marble oval slab with dark border. Urn with foliated body and handles and double conoid lid with flambeau, standing on a plain base with heraldic badge and supported with console brackets flanked by emblems of an hour-glass and a sun-burst, all on a slab with fluted edge which is on a curved faced and sided memorial panel which finishes with gathered palm-leaf base.
This is a particularly carefully drawn design. It is one of the two chosen for illustration by Dening in his *Eighteenth Century Architecture of Bristol* where he says it is by William.
Mr R. Winpenny's memorial in All Saints Church (1799) by William Paty. There is also a coarsened and reduced edition of it in Westbury Parish Church, to James Lewis which is dated 1800 and is unsigned.
Inscribed. 4
IL
60/-

William Paty/Thomas and Sons

4

4. Wove paper. 147 × 207.
Black ink and grey wash. A grey (slate) oval background on which is a white lidded and stemmed urn with palm leaves on the lower half. A band, below the lid, is drawn in perspective and has a ring of discs. The urn stands on a low base which is on a cornice to a semi-oval plaque intended for the memorial message.
No inscription.
A monument in St. James' Church to the Rev. Thomas Payne A.M. who died in 1777 dates this to the very beginning of the Thomas Paty and Sons era. There is also a monument in SS Philip and Jacob.

Thomas Paty and Sons. or Thomas Paty.

5

5. Wove paper, cut to oval 112 × 185.
Ink, grey wash and watercolour. Similar to 4 above but more attenuated. Urn has a knop at top and a heraldic badge at the waist with a rampant lion on azure ground below three stars on a gold ground. A motto reads *Nisi Dominus Prustra*.
Two copies are in St. Michael's Church: one to Hugh Inglis, dated 1796, with the badge as drawn, is unsigned; and the other, dated 1797 to William Keats, has a different badge and is signed by William Paty.

William Paty.

6

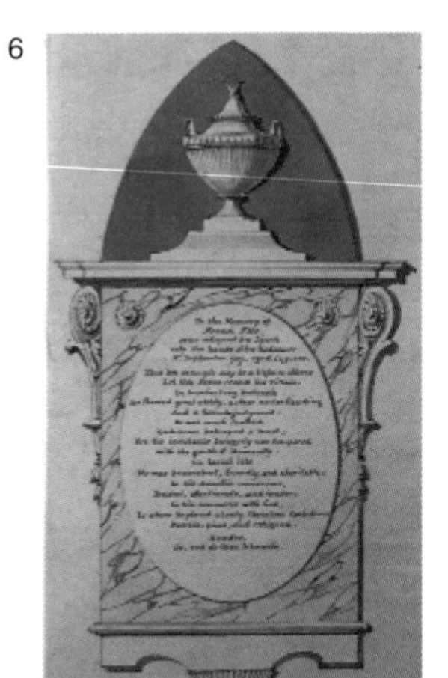

6. Wove paper. 125 × 225.
Ink, grey wash, watercolour. Monument to Peter Fry at Axbridge Parish Church. A rare example of a design that is positively identified. (There are five others, one of which is an alternative for this (No. 71.)) The inscription is fully set out and reads:
"To the memory of Peter Fry who resigned his spirit to the hands of the redeemer 21st. September, 1787 aged 52 years. That his example may be a light to others let this stone record his virtues. In transacting business he showed great ability, a clear understanding and a sound judgement. He was much trusted and never betrayed a trust, yet his inviolable integrity was tempered with the gentlest humanity. In social life he was benevolent, friendly and charitable, in his domestic connexions prudent, affectionate and tender. In his commerce with God in whom he placed a truly Christian confidence, Humble Pious and Resigned.

Reader.

Go and do thou Likewise."

An oval white plaque bears the above message. It is on a coloured marble rectangular panel with two paterae at the top. A white shaped base in the form of opposing brackets springing from a floriate fan. The classical cornice is stepped at the ends to accommodate beautifully drawn console brackets. Above, is a carved, lidded, simple urn on a stand, with foliage handles all on a grey curve-sided pyramidal background.
The actual monument at Axbridge has a different urn, more like that on No. 71 and the base is also different but there is a marked difference in quality between the drawings (brilliant) and the actuality (mundane, even sub-standard). The proportions of the space left between oval and surround is less satisfying, the carving of the brackets is coarse, compared to the subtle drawing, and the cornice on the monument is mean.
Thomas Paty was 75 years old then. The difference in quality between the drawings and the carving is both unusual and difficult to explain. The importance of the wealthy Quaker chocolate maker must surely have warranted the greatest of care in all respects. The monument is not signed. Was it made on his Estate to the Paty's design? See note against Nos 74 & 75 below.

Thomas Paty and Sons.

7

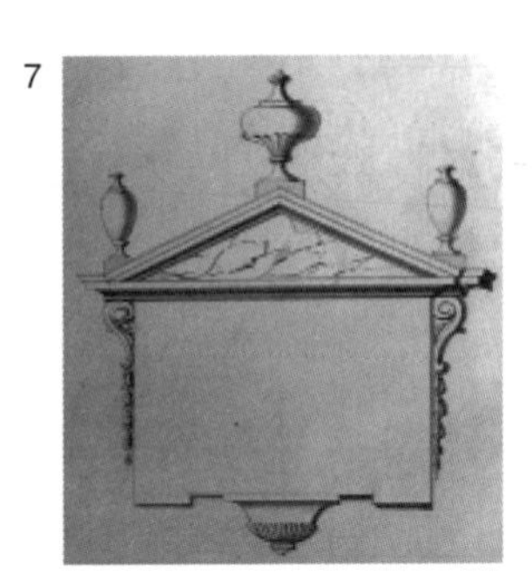

7. Laid paper. 165 × 175.
Ink and grey wash. Simple rectangular plaque with eared pediment, ears supported by consols and leaves. Two pots at extremities and an urn at the peak. Marbling drawn in the tympanum.

A similar unsigned memorial in Abbots Leigh Church is dedicated to Edmund Neale Esq., and dated 27th Oct 1745.

James Paty (2).

8. Similar to 7. above, but without consols and the pediment and cornice replaced by a simple flat triangle on a cornice, an urn at the centre. Rough pencil note for the addition of a heraldic badge and foliage at the base which is expanded in size.

James Paty (2).

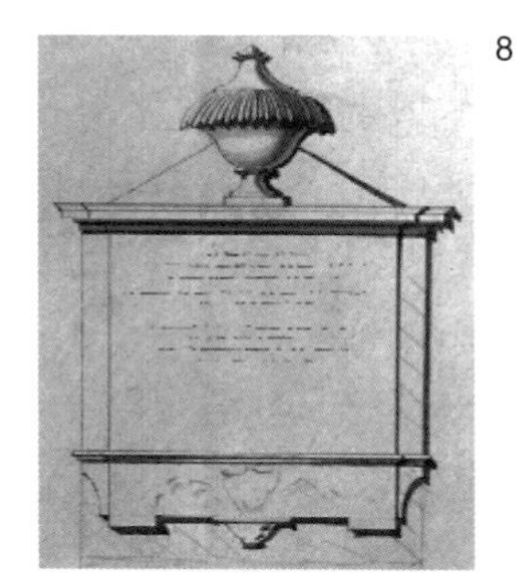

8

9. Laid paper. 190 × 310.
Ink, grey wash and watercolour. A white memorial slab with curved top on a coloured marble background on a shaped coloured marble base with brackets and a cornice. Foliated brackets at the top support a second, larger cornice on which stands an urn with foliated base, a broad waist-band and a decorated lidded top. All on a high marble pyramid adorned with a draped, knotted swag.
Memorial to John Bowland M.A. 1764. St John's, City. Unsigned.

Thomas Paty.

9

10. Laid paper. 125 × 240. Watermark indistinguishable. Ink, grey wash. Sepia ink. A framed white plaque on a grey marble background with an eared curved base on which are a heraldic badge and foliage supporters. A cornice above and a curve sided pyramid with pointed apex on which is an elongated handled and lidded urn. A pair of paterae flank the urn.
The sepia ink work is additional. It includes dimensions to the white plaque, an inscription to "John Howell" and the signature "Wood" on a drawing by

Thomas Paty.

11. Laid paper. 198 × 250. Ink and grey wash. An oval white slab on a grey (slate) rectangular background. A white base that is eared and finished in the middle with a palm leaf fan. A full cornice above holds a tall urn on a base in front of a slate curved, stepped and reverse curved backing. Inscribed "Ab't £28.10." and a cut-off signature of Wood.
This was a popular model which appears in St Philip and Jacob, St Michael's, St Thomas's and the Cathedral where one is dedicated to Rev. Thomas Merriot.DD. 1781.

Thomas Paty and Sons.

12. Wove paper. 136 × 264. Ink and grey wash. Rectangular memorial plaque on slate background flanked with pilaster strips decorated with foliate swags and with cap of plain block with a patera. The base has a continuous moulded band above a multi-curved panel with heraldic badge and foliage. On top, over a classical cornice, an urn fronting a double curved backing slab. Inscribed "No 90" plus a blot and "Wood, Bristol" all in sepia ink. See also No 2.

Thomas Paty and Sons.

13

13. Laid paper. 150 × 230. Watermark. Crown and shield. Ink, brown ink, grey wash, watercolour. Rectangular memorial slab with set-back sides to form pilasters in marble. A straight cornice, a marble pediment without cornice. At the centre an ovoid urn with a broad central reeded band. The base, drawn as grey and white marble, is contained within simple brackets that support the underside of the pilasters over, contains a heraldic badge in a floriate wreath.
Inscribed in faint pencil "the choice for Robert? Stuart? Priest? Esq. Mont."

James Paty (3)?

14. Wove paper 121 × 226. Creased. Had perhaps been folded into a letter. Ink and grey wash. Vertical oval plaque on dark (slate) background. Below a simple moulding, a white base with ears and a palm-leaf fan at the centre and the name-band finished with dentilles. Above is a cornice, extended at the sides and supported with carved and crocketted consol brackets. Above the cornice an arched pyramid background for a fluted, double-curved, stemmed urn, capped with a flambeau. All on a curved plain base.
Inscribed with a tiny 50 above the top of the Pyramid. One of the Peter Fry proposals.

Thomas Paty and Sons? William Paty?

15. Laid paper. 137 × 270. Ink and grey wash. Sepia ink. Watercolour. Vague pencil notes below. White rectangle with segmental base and segmental dentil at lowest point. Plain pilasters at side with elongated urn brackets that are fluted and tapered and with dependant leaf sprigs on them. On this a classical cornice and an ogee shaped pyramid of grey marble is background to a squat, stemmed and lidded plain urn carrying a heraldic badge with a red reversed chevron.

Thomas Paty?

16. Laid paper. 192 × 253. Sepia/indian ink wash. Identical with No. 11 above except that the background dark (slate) is shown here as black and the urn on this sits directly onto the cornice over the oval plaque whilst in No. 11. it sits on a curved sided base.
Inscribed. No. 2 in sepia ink, scratched out. Pencil inscription also rubbed out and indecipherable except (possibly) "Passmore" and "Wales".
This was a standard William Paty design as it had been a Thomas and Sons one. St. Thomas Church. Mr. Berjew. Signed. William Paty. Westbury Parish Church. James Cross. 1791. Signed William Paty.

William Paty.

17. Wove paper. 89 × 204. Sepia ink. Grey wash. Watercolour. Vertical oval plaque on grey marble slab with eared top sides and a segmental bottom under which is a heraldic badge with foliated branches as supporters. The main plaque is draped with foliage, too, tied with ribbon at the top. A neat cornice and a grey marble curved and reverse curved backing for an enclosed urn with palm leaves on lower section, a broad centre band and a top with flambeau.
St. Stephen's. Robt. Howe, 1830.

Henry Wood. But the drawing may be T. Paty.

18. Laid paper. 194 × 236. Watermark. d r. Sepia ink and wash. Marble background with broken pediment supported on voluted pilasters capped with blocks decorated with paterae. Base moulding is stepped forward at the pilasters and a support block is finished with a gathered palm leaf cluster which complement a similar central feature. A vertical oval plaque is draped with foliated branches. Above the broken pediment at the centre is a wide-waisted and lidded urn flanked by a pair of stemmed, long oval urns with lids, resting on the slope of the pediment over the pilaster strips.
A rather old-fashioned design and gauche.

James Paty (2)?

18

19. Heavy laid paper. 180 × 280. Sepia ink. Grey wash. Horizontal plain slab with horizontal oval memorial slab on it. Edge strips recessed to form sort of negative pilaster strips in grey/white marble. A segmental and eared base with simplified brackets to support the negative pilaster strips above, all in marble. Above a cornice, a tall pyramid in grey marble with the top cut off, as backing for a tall ovoid urn with palm leaves around the top half, below an ogee lid. Urn stands on a

tall plinth with bracket-shaped sides. The plinth supports an heraldic badge in a rococo frame.

Thomas Paty.

20

20. Heavy laid paper. 148 × 198. Ink and grey wash. Plain rectangular memorial slab on marbled backing. Edges recessed to form pilasters with paterae as capitals. Moulded edges and with ribbons and foliate 'tails' down the centre of the pilasters. Segmental eared and bracketted base but with a large patera supported by foliage in centre. Above, a full cornice and pediment with marbled tympanum capped with 3 urns similar to No. 18 above but here the pediment is eared, giving an unclassical and incorrect feel to the whole, but providing a more secure base for the outer pots. Central pot is wide as in No. 18 but with a wide neo-classical middle band decorated with paterae and arcading and with handles. The lid is finished with palm leaves and a flambeau.

James Paty (2)?

21. Laid paper. 127 × 228. Watermark. Shield. Ink and grey wash. Drawing has been folded once, across the middle. Vertical oval memorial slab on marble backing with ears left and right and segmental projection at base. Cornice above and curved backing finished as a pointed arch form as background for a tall cup-shaped, stemmed urn with a tall lid topped with a knop. The urn stands on a shaped plinth.

Thomas Paty.

22

22. Wove paper. 181 × 209. Black ink and grey wash. Black ink wash as a rectangular slate or marble backing. White rectangular memorial slab flanked by a pair of downward tapering pilasters with three black volutes. Pilasters have bracket bases between which is a base with ears and a curved centre on which is a beribboned group of bamboo stalks. At the top, a neo-classical cornice on which sits a stemmed shallow and wide fluted urn with flambeaux as handles, a shallow lid with fluting, a dome and a flambeau.
A very modern, neo classical design.

Perhaps Henry Wood.

23. Laid paper 225 × 280. Ink, grey wash, watercolour. Vertical rectangle memorial slab on coloured marble background with white pilaster strips with paterae as capitals and decorated with hanging leafage. Base moulding and a curved base between blocks under the pilasters. Base, stepped, curved and decurved on which is an heraldic badge in an oval shield with palm leaves as

supporters. Above a straight cornice, black slate/marble stepped, curved and decurved background for a tall ovoid stemmed urn with lid. A laurel leaf band at the wide point. Palm leaves below and on stem. A plain top with fluted and leaved lid.

Thomas Paty? William Paty?

24. Laid paper. 142 × 220. Ink, grey wash and watercolour. Plain vertical rectangular memorial slab on coloured marble backing. Simple base moulding and eared and segmental fan form at base. Cornice above, extended at the sides to accommodate a handsome pair of consol brackets. Over the cornice, an arched grey slate backing for neat stemmed and lidded urn with body decorated with palm leaves, a broad band decorated with oak leaves at centre and lid with neck band and floriate top. All on a curved sided plinth on a base. A Peter Fry variant with rectangular memorial slab.

William or Thomas Paty.

24

25. Wove paper. 148 × 215. Ink, grey wash and watercolour. Grey washed (slate) background with arched head and segmental base encloses the whole monument except for the bottom (sculptor's name) bracket. A coloured marble slab encloses the memorial rectangle. Pilaster strips either side, capped with paterae. Simple base mould. Plain pilaster bases below, finished with gathered palm-leaf ends; between them a larger edition of the same but with vine leaves and grapes to complete. Above, the top member of the cornice is finished with fluting. Above it a tall stemmed and lidded urn with half the main curved body with palm leaves. At the middle, a broad decorated band and above it a plain lid that is tapered, completed with a foliate cap with knop. Above this, below the peak of the background, a heraldic shield with pampas grass supporters. This drawing is inscribed "W. Paty, Bristol" at the base, where the monument would be inscribed. Although it is quite similar to the two previous drawings it is somewhat tenuous by comparison. Could this be an early example of William's work? Other inscriptions are: Top left in pencil. D.R. Bottom left in pencil. 7–3.

William Paty.

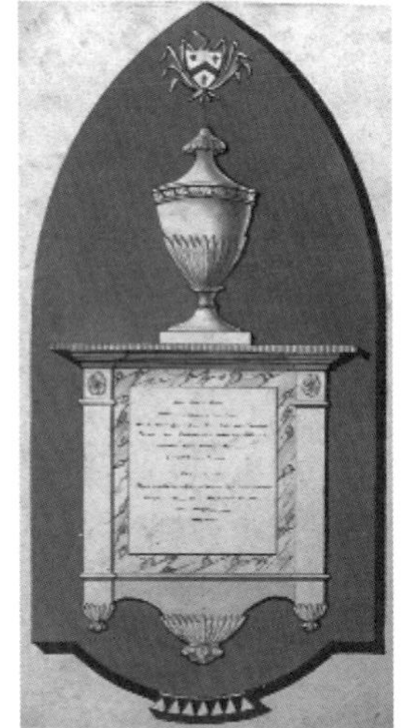
25

26. Laid paper. 115 × 196. Ink, grey wash. The memorial slab as a drapery, tied in bows at the top corners, knotted at the centre, top and hanging loose at the bottom. Skilfully drawn with a suggestion that the surface of the slab itself is rippled. The slab is on a marbled background which has a segmental base that follows

approximately the line of the bottom of the slab. Above, a cornice and a marbled background of same width as main background develops into an arch-shaped pyramid on which is a curved and eared plinth with heraldic badge in a flourish on which is a tall, lidded urn. Excellent draughtsmanship and fine detailing.

Thomas Paty.

27

27. Wove paper. 220 × 305. An almost square memorial slab with black edge strips at the sides and with grey marbling at top and bottom. Above, and matching the width of the memorial slab, a plain chest shaped "sarcophagus" on short legs with triangular side panels, The lid projects to the edge of the monument and forms a cornice on which sits a broad, carefully detailed, stemmed and lidded urn, boldly gadrooned on the lower half of its cup shape. Top edge with a rim of laurel leaves. A shallow lid rises in the centre to a bold neck and knop. The black background is shouldered immediately above the top of the "sarcophagus" and completed in a segmental arched top, enclosing the urn. The drawing is carefully carried out with shadows and highlights carefully considered. The design corresponds to the Harriet Ducarel monument, dated 1815 and not signed, in Bristol Cathedral.
Inscribed in pencil at top L to R. "540. 5.2–3.2 620."

Henry Wood.

28

28. Laid paper. 237 × 407. J. Whatman (watermark). Watered ink, grey wash, raw sienna wash within a frame of two lines. An old-fashioned baroque design for a very three-dimensional wall monument. A plain rectangular memorial slab on a bulbous bolection curved casket with gadrooning on the lower and with etched decoration at the shoulder. The casket and the slab rest on a base with an ovolo and below it a large shallow cyma-recta base whose surface is decorated with acanthus leaves. This, supported on a mourning cherub's head with wings. Above the casket and slab a cornice, plinth, a narrowing decurved shaft with shield, ribbons and roses in a garland around the shield and down the sides of the plinth. Above, another cornice or cap-mould forming the base for another (bolection moulded) plinth for a stemmed closed urn with the main cup of the tall shape cut to three arched niches in which are cherubs' heads with wings closely folded under them. The lid of the urn is finished with a flambeau. Shadows on the drawing indicate that the urn is fully three dimensional. This bold and vigorous design is, with No. 92 below, probably by James Paty (1). It is one of the few baroque designs in the copybook. As with No 92, the draughtsmanship is

powerful and quite different to Thomas and William. It is a great pity that the Whatman paper was not dated. It is pre the wove hot-pressed, apparently, with an old typeface in the watermark.

James Paty (1).

29. Laid paper 120 × 220 (extremes of drawing) which is cut out. Ink, grey wash, yellow wash and watercolour. Vertical oval memorial slab on a plain marble backing with raw sienna wash over marbling making it stand out from the rest of the monument which is without wash. The slab flanked by recessed strips capped with moulding and blocks with paterae. The base has a well detailed cap-mould. Under the pilaster strips are a pair of plain brackets on each side and a pair of triglyphs under the main background and, in the centre, a plain slab with a segmental projection. Above, a cornice and a large plinth that extends the full width of the monument and which curves up to ears and a cap-moulding. The plinth carries a baroque heraldic shield with supporting acanthus leaves and floriat swags. Above the cap-mould, a plain, broad stemmed urn with a broad, fluted waist-band and a lid with a spiked top.

Thomas Paty.

30. Laid paper. 213 × 250. Ink, grey wash and watercolour. Rectangular memorial slab with base cut to large segment (almost semi-circular) on shoulders. The background of coloured marble is similarly shaped and has pilaster strips with paterae 'capitals' and long floral drapes and has a base of palm-leaf cones. A simple cornice forms the base for a grey marble double curved and shouldered backing for a stemmed tall, lidded urn with a broad waist-band. Palm leaves decorate the body and the tall lid which is finished with a floriate knob. Inscribed, top left in pencil "5–3
I X"

Thomas Paty.

31. Detail paper 400 × 250 + old transparent tape. Watermark. J. Whatman 1833. Pencil outline drawing of a broad-lidded funerary urn with handles in the form of acroteria. The rim of the urn is fluted, the base completed by acanthus leaves taken down to a moulded ring at the lower edge of the paper. The urn would have been completed with a stem below.
This drawing is the most recent of all those in the book and post-dates all the known draughtsmen (Henry Wood died in 1828). It is either a working drawing or a student's drawing, but probably the former as the

drawing goes right to the edge of the paper, although there is no evidence that the drawing has been traced or "pricked through".

Anon.

32

32. Laid paper 218 × 280. Ink, grey wash. Horizontal rectangle for memorial stone flanked by consol brackets, all on a plain marble base which stands on a moulded cornice standing on a marble plain segment and shouldered base, flanked by a pair of triglyphs and a pair of unmoulded brackets. Above the memorial slab, a main cornice on which is a block-plinth in grey marble on which is a tall slab in the same marble in several curves, terminating in a semi-circle. On this, a tall, stemmed, and lidded urn with a broad moulded waist and a flambeau top. Above this, a heraldic badge of baroque shape and with a flourish of leaves as supporters. A crest of an arm and fist, wielding what looks like a pen or a paintbrush.
This design is old fashioned, probably from the first half of the century.

James Paty (1) or early Thomas.

33. Laid paper. 140 × 216. Indecipherable watermark. Vertical rectangle memorial slab but with segmental base. Flanked with pilasters decorated with ribbons and floral drapes. Pilasters finished at base with cup-shaped brackets. Above, a simple cornice, a grey, low double-curved backing for a stemmed, lidded funerary urn with handles and a broad waist with laurel wreath.
The paper is cut through with a razor along the top.
Inscribed in pencil top left "CA as" top right "AE c" bottom left "6.4–3.4." bottom right "4.4–2.4"

Thomas Paty? and Sons?

34

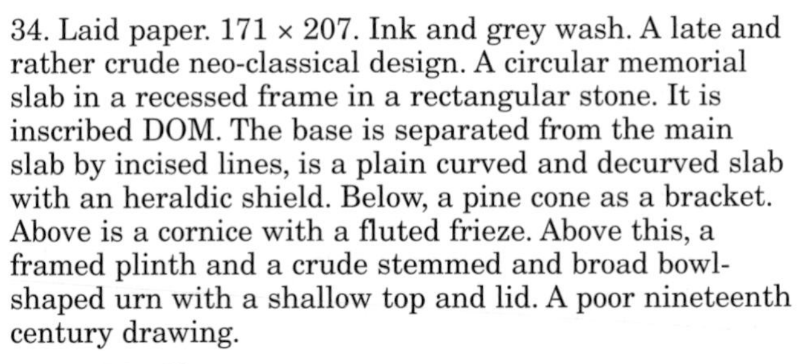

34. Laid paper. 171 × 207. Ink and grey wash. A late and rather crude neo-classical design. A circular memorial slab in a recessed frame in a rectangular stone. It is inscribed DOM. The base is separated from the main slab by incised lines, is a plain curved and decurved slab with an heraldic shield. Below, a pine cone as a bracket. Above is a cornice with a fluted frieze. Above this, a framed plinth and a crude stemmed and broad bowl-shaped urn with a shallow top and lid. A poor nineteenth century drawing.

Henry Wood?

35. Wove paper. 177 × 237. Ink, grey wash, Indian ink wash and watercolour. A rectangular memorial slab with a segmentally projecting base on a coloured marble

backing. Flanking pilaster strips capped with paterae and with palm-leaf bases. Pilasters carry graded leaf garlands. Below the segmental base, a heraldic shield with opening fans as supporters. Above, a cornice and a black, double curved background for a simple plinth and a stemmed wide urn with palm leaves, a broad, decorated waist-band and a lid crowned with palm leaves and handles. Inscribed in pencil across the top, L to R "612. 4.0–2.7. 6–3. 900."

Thomas Paty or Thomas Paty and Sons.

36. Laid paper. 260 × 260. Indecipherable watermark. Ink and grey wash. Similar in design and draughtsmanship to No. 34 above. Rectangular memorial slab with corners cut away at top with circular studs in them and at the base, similar studs supporting the slab. Shallow segment cut away at base, between the studs to make extra room for the heraldic badge and its supporters of leaf and laurel leaf with crossed bones beneath. A pair of consol brackets at the outside edges and a cone with oak leaves at the centre as base. Above the frame which surrounds the memorial slab, a narrow strip, which is also framed, containing three paterae and draped floral swags. Above this a cornice on which stand three blocky plinths, the centre one supporting a dish-shaped urn on stem with a plain waist band and an open, narrowed top, from which flames arise. As in No. 34 above, the memorial slab has D.O.M. as a main element. This is a better drawing than No. 34 and a much bolder design but still remarkably crude.

Henry Wood?

36

37. Laid paper. 216 × 282. Ink, grey wash, watercolour. Tall rectangular memorial slab flanked by ionic pilasters, deeply fluted with a full classical entablature with architrave, pulvinated frieze and pedimented cornice surmounted with three urns. The pilasters are flanked with narrow strips of coloured marble which allow a horizontal projection of the cornice beyond the pediment. Below, a base moulding and a shaped, curved base on which is a heraldic badge in a baroque flourish.
Inscriptions. In pencil, a section? of a church showing the position of a pew relative to the wall and an x mark in sepia ink. In sepia ink a note: "If two of these monuments are placed by each other they must be rais'd on account of the pew mark'd X projecting forward on the space, as in this place there is not sufficient room to receive them without touching each other."

James Paty (1).

37

38

38. Laid paper. 223 × 287. Ink and grey wash. Vertical rectangular memorial slab but with shallow segmental bite out of top and acanthus-leaved brackets left and right top corners onto frieze and cornice of broken pediment. A baroque heraldic badge in centre, rising into tympanum through the broken pediment, which is surmounted by a fat stemmed and waisted and lidded urn with two tall urns at the sides. Memorial slab flanked with narrow marble strips, widened at the foot onto a plinth above a cornice to the base member in marble, which is shaped, curved and bracketted.
This drawing, the previous one and the following one (37, 38, 39) all appear to be by the same draughtsman. There are two editions of it in All Saints' Church and another in Henbury Parish Church, the first two, to two members of the Freeman family, dated 1764 and 1766, one of them signed J. Paty, and the latter to Anne Smyth dated 1760 and unsigned. All are without the central urn.

James Paty (1) via Rachel Paty his widow.

39. Laid paper. 210 × 285. Ink and grey wash. Vertical rectangular memorial slab with narrow recessed pilaster strips each side. Flat cornice, a plinth in marble with baroque heraldic badge on a curved marble background which narrows to the top. Completed with a second cornice on which is a funeral urn stemmed with a fluted base, a broad waist-band and a tall conical lid with a floral knob. The base below is eared and rectilinear with plain brackets at each side. Inscribed. Centre, top in sepia ink. "No. 2".

James Paty (1).

40

40. Laid paper. 228 × 352. Watermark. J. Whatman. Ink, grey wash, Chinese ink. A grand monument, grandly drawn. Stylistically, R Adam, neo-classical. An upright rectangular memorial slab between pilaster strips formed with capitals of enclosed laurel wreaths over framed panels containing ribbon at top, supporting a string of leaves, a laurel leaf garland and a pair of cornucopia, crossed. A base moulding and, below, blocks gathered with clustered palm leaves underneath the pilasters, and a curved base slab gathered into a fan-shaped fluting at the centre. At the top, the pilasters and memorial slab are completed with a cornice on which sits a black, tall curving pyramid which supports an elegant tall, stemmed and lidded funerary urn decorated with palm leaves, swags with ribbons and a bold linked-chains waist band. The urn sits on a plinth with heraldic badge in a flourish. Flanking this, a pair of consol brackets delicately carved all on a plain plinth. This design was for Abraham Elton's monument in Wells Cathedral

cloister, except that the pyramid is a Gothic arch and the memorial slab is converted to a horizontal rectangle there.

Dated 1794 and signed, William Paty.

41. Wove paper. 166 × 200. Ink and grey wash. Horizontal, rectangular memorial slab with segmental projection at the base. Flanked with fluted pilasters capped with paterae with bases formed with curved corbels. Above, a cornice and a curved, stepped and curved marble backing for a broad, stemmed and lidded urn which is decorated with a garland of leaves draped over the waist-band of the urn and down on either side to end above the tops of the pilasters.
Similar to a memorial in Westbury on Trym Parish Church to James Morgan dated 1780 and signed by Thomas Paty and Sons.

Thomas Paty and Sons.

42. Wove paper. 165 × 200. Ink and grey wash and watercolour. Horizontal oval memorial slab on coloured marble backing eared at top and segmental below, following line of memorial oval. Circular paterae left and right. Straight classical cornice, a curved, stepped and curved grey marble backing to a stemmed and lidded, broad funerary urn with a boldly gadrooned top and swagged garlands below. Inscribed in pencil, top left. "ER".

Thomas Paty.

43. Wove paper. 230 × 270. top right corner torn off. Ink, grey wash, watercolour. Memorial slab in the form of a bolection-mould casket with a cast shadow to demonstrate its three-dimensionality. Flanked by coloured marble slightly recessed but continuing the bolection shape. Below, a simple base moulding, a pair of acanthus-leaved brackets under the corners of the memorial slab. Flanked with plain bracket shapes L and R and enclosing coloured marble centrepiece with segmental base and with a baroque heraldic badge in a flourish. Above, a cornice with a curved broken pediment. The curves in wave form and finished with foliate paterae. The space enclosed by the pediment protects the foot of a large, tall funerary urn which is egg-shaped, standing on a stem, has a bold waist decorated with paterae and flutes in groups of three and a gadrooned top on which sits the tall lid. A strong laurel leaf garland is tied at the waist-band, drapes over the pot and falls to the tops of the curved broken pediment whose line it follows downwards. A grand bold baroque

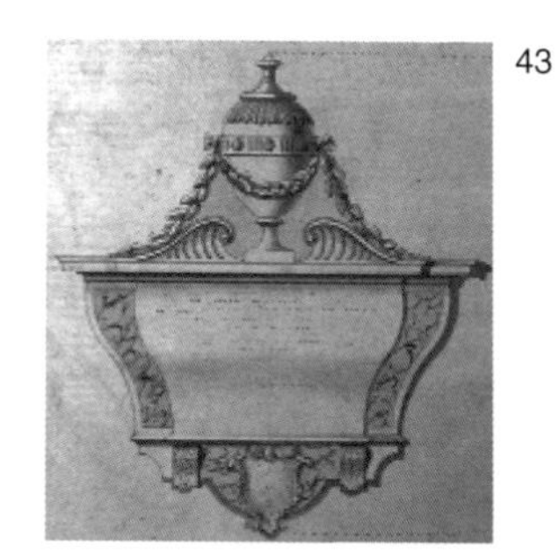
43

44

45

46

design. Corresponds to a monument in Westbury Parish Church to William Phelps dated 1764 which is apparently not signed.
Inscribed. Sepia ink measurement dotted line from top and bottom extremities and note "Heigth 7 feet". An illegible pencil note may contain the name "Phelps". There are also two pencil emendations to the form of the urn.

Thomas Paty.

44. Laid paper. 271 × 360. Watermark. Shield and "G R". Vertical oval memorial slab on coloured marble backing which has outcurving feet. Four draped circular paterae at the corners and a ribbon appears to carry the slab at the top. The marble backing is flanked at the top with a pair of carved consol brackets from which laurel-leaved garlands are suspended. At the base, a pair of egg-shaped tall urns on stems. Below, a base moulding, a front elevation and a side elevation of brackets on either side and in the centre, a segmental projection filled with a heraldic badge in a flourish of palm leaves. Above, a broken classical pediment on an architrave in white marble. Architrave plain and open to the tympanum where hangs a draped and knotted cloth. Above the tympanum a broad-stemmed and lidded urn draped with a floral garland each side which descends to the top of the pediment.

Thomas Paty.

45. Wove paper. 166 × 260. Ink and grey wash, watercolour. Memorial slab in form of draped cloth knotted at top corners and draped around the head of a winged cherub at centre top. On a coloured marble backing with an open segmental cornice above the cherub and above it a tall stemmed and lidded urn with palm leaves on the lower half of the cup and a garland around paterae on the urn which is then draped down to the top of the pediment. A handsome consol bracket on each side supports a horizontal extension of the cornice with garlands below. A base moulding at the bottom with a pair of tapered, fluted brackets L and R and a central curved base-member with heraldic badge and acanthus leaves as support.

Thomas Paty.

46. Laid paper. 165 × 248. Ink and grey wash and watercolour. Horizontal oval memorial slab on rectangular coloured marble slab with projecting feet. Flanked with recessed strips eared and decorated with paterae and garlands, stopped at the base with toothing.

At the top, a classical cornice and a grey-washed curved and stepped and arched pyramid, against which stands a curve plinth capped with palm leaves on which sits a tall stemmed and lidded urn with handles. The cup of the urn is decorated with swags tied with ribbons.

William Paty.

47

47. Laid paper. 122 × 224. Ink, grey wash and watercolour. Horizontal oval memorial slab on rectangular coloured marble background with circular paterae at top corners. Oval slab draped with leaf garlands, tied with ribbons. Below, a base course and base slab, eared corners and central palm-leaf cluster. Above, a cornice and a tall arch-shaped pyramid of grey marble against which rests a small rectangular plinth with knotted loop of drapery. Plinth supported with consol brackets. On this, a tall stemmed urn with fluted lid, handles and a draped garland.

William Paty.

48

48. Laid paper 208 × 246 Watermark. Crown and shield. Ink, grey wash and water-colours. Vertical oval with garlands over top on a coloured marble base with segmental projection on top into a segmental cornice. Lower corners eared and with garlanded circular paterae. At the top sides, a pair of garlanded consol brackets support the ends of the cornice. A base moulding and below, a pair of acanthus-leaved consol brackets flanked by eared blocks enclose a double curved slab which contains a cherub's head and extended wings and clouds. Above the cornice, a grey marble double curved and stepped grey marble backing to a short-stemmed pot with a broad fluted waist-band. Fluting and draped cloths on the lower part of the pot and a plain low conoid lid with a foliated knob. Palm-leaf supporters.
This design was illustrated in C.F.W. Dening's *Eighteenth Century Architecture of Bristol* 1923, Plate 1. where it is attributed to William Paty.

Thomas Paty.

These last five drawings appear together on a single spread of the copybook and are worth special notice because they demonstrate as clearly as anywhere the differences between William and Thomas as designers and draughtsmen. Numbers 44, 45, and 48 are here attributed to Thomas and are dateable to mid-century and are full of baroque motifs. There are two segmental cornices and one broken pediment, two cherubs' heads, bold consol brackets are used in all three and garlands and drapery is much used. Numbers 46 and 47, on the

other hand, are less cluttered, have a reduced number of elements and the pots/urns are more emphatically used and are the most important element of the design. They are elegantly neo-classical and are meant to represent Robert Adam in Bristol.
In terms of draughtsmanship, the five drawings are much more difficult to separate and indeed many might suggest that there are no significant differences detectable. The ruled and freehand penmanship is remarkably similar as is the application of shadow and background washes, but there are subtle tricks in the way of recording specific features that allow one to trace a different hand at work. Thomas loved cherubs and draperies and he drew them in a way that demonstrated that love, whilst his descriptions of pots demonstrated a lack of concern about them and their status in his scheme. They could be left out of these designs without destroying the design. In Nos. 46 and 47 however, the removal of the pots would destroy the design. The draughtsmanship shows how dedicated to the neo-classical William was and how much he concentrated upon its careful depiction. These two designs show a level of sophistication which was new, was demonstrably end-of-the-century and up-to-the-minute.

49

49. Laid paper. 248 × 313. Ink, grey wash and watercolour. A vertical oval grey marble slab. On it, a half-oval memorial slab on another coloured marble backing. A straight cornice on which is a shallow plinth and on that a rectangular podium flanked with decorated consol brackets. On the podium, paired heraldic badges and foliate supporters. Another cornice on which a tall stemmed and lidded funerary urn, decorated with a garland draped over the left shoulder of the top of the urn and around its body. Lid is reeded, with a beaded neck and a floriate top. Waist-band with laurel leaves, lower half of body with palm leaves. Inscribed in sepia ink on the drawing is "Wood Bristol" and bottom right, "Hy Wood Bristol" although this is undoubtedly a William Paty drawing.

William Paty.

50

50. Laid paper. 118 × 240. Ink, grey wash and watercolour. Memorial slab as a curved-sided casket but without any modelling, flanked with coloured marble strips that follow the same lines. This all sits on a moulded base under which is a pair of triglyphs with plain brackets outside them and a segmentally curved base slab in coloured marble. Above, a cornice, stepped forward over the memorial slab, and over this an S-curved baroque broken pediment with a tall, stemmed,

lidded ovoid funerary urn between the arms of the pediment. A garland, fixed to the middle of the urn and draped round it is taken down to the top of the broken pediment. All this on a tall curved grey marble pyramid. An heraldic badge with palm leaves above the urn. This appears to be a composite design, with the main, lower part typically Thomas and the upper (urn and pyramid) William.

Thomas Paty and Sons.

51

51. Wove paper. 123 × 240. Cut to arch shape. Ink grey wash and watercolour. Rectangular memorial slab with pilaster strips of coloured marble topped with moulding and paterae. Base moulding, triglyphs and grey marble double curved base slab. Above, a flat cornice, topped with a curved and eared plinth, decorated with heraldic badge and palm-leaved supporters and finished with a second cornice and a tall ovoid urn as in No. 50 above, garlanded on the pot and down to the corners of the top of the plinth. Similar ambiguity of design to the last example.

Thomas Paty and Sons.

52

52. Laid paper. 155 × 242. Has been twice folded into a letter. Ink, grey wash and watercolour. Closely similar to No. 51 above except that the rectangular memorial slab is replaced by a vertical oval slab on a coloured marble background with eared corners and circular paterae at the top corners. Faint pencil outline for an amended top.

Thomas Paty and Sons.

53

53. Laid paper. 150 × 250. Ink and grey wash. Horizontal oval memorial slab on grey marble backing flanked with tall consol brackets which support triglyph (actually quatroglyph) "capitals". Below, a base moulding and eared curved and decurved base in grey marble. Above, a straight cornice with grey curved, stepped and decurved backing on which is a stemmed and lidded, tall funerary urn with a cloth drape fixed to the urn with paterae. This drawing is on an unusual paper with a slight greenish tinge. The draughtsmanship is different: bolder than the usual but rather careless. At No 69 below, William (probably) makes two rough sketches to illustrate alternative designs but they are quite different.

James Paty (3)?

54. Laid paper. 202 × 222. Ink, grey wash and watercolour. Vertical oval memorial slab on coloured marble background with projecting feet, consol brackets

54

with suspended garlands and supporting "bi-glyphs" on either side. Circular paterae at bottom corners and a pair of linen drapes above, tied with ribbons and knots, taken into the tympanum of a broken pediment. Above the pediment a broad urn with extended handles at the mouth, topped with a low palm-leafed lid. A garland is draped around the eared handles across the urn and down to the top of the pediment. Base moulding and curved base with triglyphs L and R. Base decorated with crossed horn and flambeau on a serpent grasping its tail.

Thomas Paty and Sons.

55. Laid paper. 214 × 262. Ink and grey wash. Repeat with minor variations of No.s 44 and 66.

Thomas Paty.

56. Wove paper. 194 × 285. Ink, grey wash and watercolour. Similar to No. 51 but with an arched grey marble backing to podium and garlanded urn and the whole contained in another arched top backing which is finished below the monument with a shallow ogee and plain brackets L and R. This additional backing indicated with ink outline and a subtle yellow wash.

Thomas Paty and Sons/William Paty.

57. Laid paper. 115 × 285. Ink, grey wash and watercolour. Another variant of No. 51.

Thomas Paty and Sons/William Paty.

58

58. Laid paper. 200 × 285. Ink and grey wash and watercolour wash. Rectangular memorial slab on coloured marble backing flanked by pilaster strips with volutes as capitals and with the shafts decorated with leaf garlands. Base moulding with block bases under pilasters finished with clustered palm leaves. Between these a curved base slab with a central fan cluster. Above, a straight cornice, an arched grey curved pyramid on which is a very shallow podium and a stemmed and lidded broad urn with garlands, handles, palm leaves and a fluted lid.

Thomas Paty and Sons/William Paty.

59. Wove paper. 175 × 250. Ink, grey wash and watercolour. Horizontal rectangle memorial slab on coloured marble backing flanked by large consol brackets and segmental base and acanthus-leaved brackets. Lightly drawn grey veining and a shield centre. Above, a cornice, a narrow plinth band and a tall, complex shaped "pyramid" in grey marble on which is a wide, stemmed

and lidded funerary urn with a laurel-leaved waist band. Over it a marble drape suspended from bows at centre and sides.
Pencil inscription "Dove" with indicator line to the base of the monument.

Thomas Paty and Sons.

60. Laid paper. 205 × 270. Ink, grey wash and watercolour.
Repeat of No.s 51, 56, 57.

Thomas Paty.

61. Laid paper. Cut out design. 130 × 220. Rectangular memorial slab with segmental projecting base on a coloured marble backing of similar shape. Above, a cornice and a curved grey marble pyramidal backing for a simple low plinth on which a stemmed, lidded and handled broad urn with wide waist-band with links. Body of urn carries heraldic shield and floral draped lid, with leaves. Ink smudges.

Thomas Paty and Sons.

61

62. Laid paper. 220 × 290. Ink, grey wash. Shield-shaped memorial slab with ears and pointed base upon a grey marble background whose sides take up a double curve opposed to the curve of the shield. Draped paterae at the top, below a frieze moulding. Below, a classical moulding and a shaped, double curved, plain base. Above, a classical cornice and a low podium on which stands s sturdy stemmed urn with broad waist-band decorated with a chain. A lid with broad palm leaved knop. Body of urn carries floral drapes fixed with paterae and which are carried down to the podium on either side.
A different draughtsman. James Paty (2)? (3)? see No. 53.

James Paty (3).

63. Laid paper. 200 × 275. Ink, grey wash, chinese ink. Rectangular memorial slab with segmental top. Black framed pilaster strips either side with paterae as capitals and black strip between them. Below, a plinth on a base mould. Two acanthus-leaved brackets with plain brackets outside and a plain, straight base member between. Above, a cornice and a very low podium on which a double curved and stepped grey marble pyramidal backing to a stemmed, handled and lidded urn of great elegance with a floral wreath draped over the urn handles. Inscribed top left, "640" and top right, "910".

William Paty.

63

64

64. Wove paper. 210 × 305. Ink, grey wash and watercolour. Memorial slab in the form of an ogee-sided casket with coloured marble framed strips each side. Below, a base mould, a pair of plain brackets with segmental shaped base in grey marble with a flambeau, a woodwind musical instrument and a book, crossed. Above, a cornice and a curved baroque, broken pediment with a plinth and a stemmed lidded urn draped with foliate drapery taken down to the top of the pediment. All on a grey marble background which is enclosed on either side with coloured marble eared and capped pilasters inside of which are acanthus-leaved brackets which have foliate pendants and which support a broken triangular pediment in the tympanum of which is a draped and knotted cloth. Above the pediment a large baroque heraldic badge with feet and capping and dependant foliate swags. At the corners, two tall stemmed and lidded urns.
Edward Colston Jun. Monument 1763. All Saints'.

Thomas Paty or possibly James Paty (1).

65

65. Wove paper. 255 × 320. Ink grey wash and watercolour. Rectangular memorial slab but with shouldered and semi-circular headed top. Coloured marble backing going into tympanum of broken pediment supported on triglyphs sitting on shoulders of memorial slab. Pediment has stemmed and lidded urn on middle top with foliate drapes either side and a pair of tall, stemmed lidded urns beyond on flat extensions of the pediment which are supported with consols and foliate swags which extend down most of the length of the memorial slab. The base below a classical cornice is plain, eared, rectangular marble, flanked with plain consol brackets.

Thomas Paty or possibly James Paty (1).

66. Laid paper. 242 × 335. Ink, grey wash, watercolour. Oval memorial slab on grey marble base on a plinth band which extends beyond the backing to provide a base for a pair of long, ovoid, stemmed and lidded urns. All on a classical cornice and a base which is eared, shouldered and with segmental centre zone carrying a pair of plain consols and flanked by them. Main base carries a heraldic shield supported with palm leaves. The oval memorial slab is supported with a ribbon bow at top and backing carries four circular draped paterae at the corners. On either side, decorated consol brackets with pendant foliage. Above, a simple roll moulding marks a change to a yellow/red marble frieze and tympanum with an open pediment which has a twice knotted drapery. Above the pediment, a blocked plinth as base to a

stemmed and lidded wide urn with gigantic handles from which depend floriate swags draped to the pediment. The urn lid has an ostentatious flambeau top.
Pencil inscriptions. At top "£86.0.0 if 9ft high". On the memorial slab, two dimensions "2′5″ and 3′3″. The same draughtsmanship as in No.s 64 and 65 above.

Thomas Paty or possibly James Paty (1).

67

67. Wove paper. 144 × 243. Ink, grey wash. Rectangular memorial slab on a grey background. Simple base moulding and a plain eared and shaped base onto a central fan. Either side, a decorated consol bracket with modest floral drapes suspended. Above, a classical cornice and a grey arch shaped "pyramid" as background to an elegant large, stemmed and lidded urn on a broad plinth draped with a mourning cloth; again, most elegantly drawn. Shadows are cast and, in addition, an outline of the whole monument is drawn around the whole in a lighter grey, so that three different intensities of grey wash are used. Similar to the Hester Prideaux monument, 1792. St. Michael-on-the-Mount-Without. Another variant of the Fry monument.

William Paty.

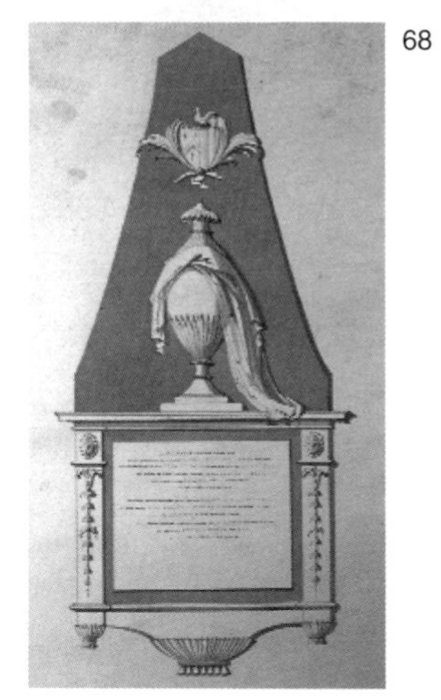
68

68. Laid paper. 255 × 355. Ink, grey wash. Horizontal rectangular memorial slab on grey background flanked with pilaster strips decorated with oval paterae as capping and with Adamesque ribboned and leaved sprays. Below, a simple roll moulding, individual blocked bases for the pilasters, finished with palm-leaf fans and a segmental plain base between them, finished with a broad, palm-leafed fan. Above, a cornice and a tall, grey, curve sided "pyramid" with gabled top on which is a tall, elegant stemmed and lidded urn with palm-leaf base to ovoid body. The urn draped with a mourning cloth suspended over the shoulder of the urn, and draped to the cornice which it overrides to the right. Above the urn, a heraldic badge and reed supporters with a cockerel as crest. Pencil inscription. Top right. 7′6″ high 3′8″ wide. £46.10s." Memorial to William Keats, 1797. St. Michael-on-the-Mount-Without. Wells Cathedral Abraham Elton, 1794 where the urn is undraped and the pyramid of Gothic shape. See also No. 40.

William Paty

69

69. Laid paper. 238 × 145. Ink and grey wash. A pair of sketches of urns at the top of an oval memorial slab. Left, with a stemmed and lidded broad handled urn with a vigorous flambeau top and a draped cloth over the

shoulder and taken down both sides to the top of the memorial slab. On the right, a similar urn but without the flambeau and draped from the handles, with leafed swags taken to an oval ring, threaded through it and suspended to match the suspension at the other end through the handle of the urn. Both are free and effective drawings.

William Paty.

70

70. Laid paper. 175 × 280. Ink, grey wash and watercolour. Horizontal rectangular memorial slab with coloured marble frame inset from edge. No base moulding and the base is set back from the memorial above to give shadow. It is curved to a gathered palm-leaf cone. Outer edges marked with dentils. Above, a simple cornice and a grey washed concave, stepped and convex curved "pyramid" on which is a plinth consisting of a narrow podium, a pair of plain brackets supporting a rectangular slab on which a heraldic badge with branched supporters is a stemmed and palm leaved, banded and lidded urn. The banding with laurel leaves. Urn draped with a cloth over the shoulders. Above the urn is a large oval sun-burst. Inscribed at top left in pencil. 6. 6–3
U. X.

Thomas Paty and Sons or William Paty.

71

71. Laid paper. 153 × 282. Ink, grey wash and watercolour. An alternative design for the Peter Fry monument at Axbridge, with the words written out again but on a rectangular slab with a shouldered and segmental top and with coloured marble sides as pilasters with paterae as caps, with double curved grey (slate) pyramidal top with an urn draped with a cloth more like the actual carved urn than No. 6 above. The monument itself is more like No. 74 and 75 below than either this one or No. 6. It is possible that No. 6 and this drawing are by Thomas Paty and that the two drawings No. 74 and 75 are by William and that he (William) was by then the better draughtsman.

Thomas Paty.

72. Wove paper. 150 × 195. Sepia ink, wash and Chinese ink. Vertical oval memorial slab on black rectangular backing. Simple base moulding. Eared and double curved black base decorated centrally with an eye within an oval sun-burst Above, a coarsely drawn cornice and a double curved low black "pyramid". A small podium on which is a stemmed, plain banded and lidded tall urn with a cloth drape. Inscriptions. The memorial message

is started with "In" in sepia ink. At top left "440". Top right. "620".

Probably Henry Wood.

73

73. Laid paper. 140 × 195. Ink and grey wash. Horizontal oval memorial slab on rectangular marble slab backing flanked with large, reversed consol brackets with paterae as the focii of the swirls. The brackets support a short run of arcaded frieze which read as capitals. Below, a base moulding and a marble base with ears and double curve to a central plain bracket flanked by plain brackets under the consols. Above, a triangular pediment with ears and a marble tympanum. At the top, a podium on which is a stemmed and lidded, broad and handled urn draped with a cloth. A pencil addition suggests a double curved and stepped "pyramid" behind this. This is similar to No 53 in form and draughtsmanship and is probably by James Paty (3).

74. Laid paper. 175 × 265. Client drawing. Ink, grey wash, Chinese ink.

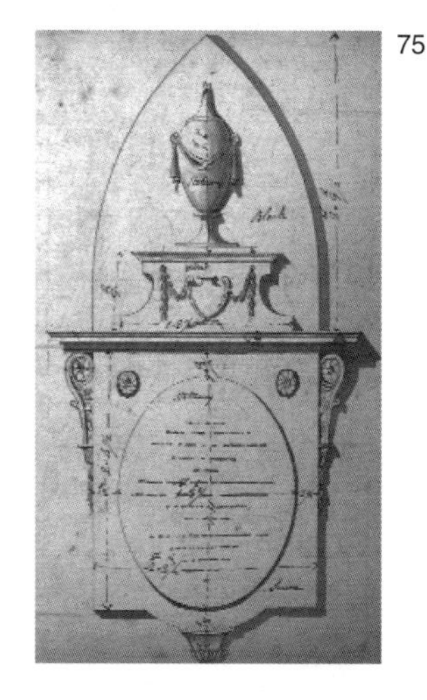
75

75. Laid paper. 160 × 243. Working drawing. Ink, grey wash.
Two drawings for the same project. It is similar to the Peter Fry monument but it does not match, but neither do No.s 6 and 71. It has a vertical oval memorial slab with two circular paterae at top R and L and has consol brackets each side with suspended leaves below. The background is black on No. 74 but is marked as "Siena" on No 75. The background is shaped at the bottom into a curved base onto a double curved bracket at the centre. Above, a classical cornice and above it a Gothic curved "pyramid" drawn in grey marble on No. 74 but marked "black" No. 75. On this, a large curved sided podium on which a baroque heraldic shield is supported with vine leaves and a ribbon of leaves, dependant from a ring to the R and L of the shoulder of the shield. Above it a cornice and on it a stemmed tall ovoid urn with tall lid. Bottom third of ovoid with fan modelling and above, draped and knotted cloth.
No. 75 is the only drawing in the book that includes detailed dimensions and notes on materials to be used. It could be that this is William or brother John showing their father what an up-to-date architect did or it could demonstrate a problem in the firm at the time of Peter Fry's burial, requiring them to issue a drawing for another craftsman to work from. This would explain how the monument itself was different from all drawings for it and also how poorly carved it was.

Thomas Paty and Sons. William/John Paty.

76

76. Wove paper. 135 × 248. Twice folded. Ink, grey wash. Grey memorial slab flanked by pilaster strips capped with moulding and oval paterae. The pilasters are decorated with dependent ribbons and leaves. Below, a simple base moulding with bases to pilaster strips, each with a four-arched frieze and a fan of palm leaves. Between them, a grey, double curved base with a large, fan-shaped white bracket. Above, a slim cornice, on which is a tall, grey curve-sided and gabled "pyramid". On it a low plinth, a rectangular podium with supporting consol brackets with a heraldic badge with reed supporters. A second cornice and shallow plinth for a tall stemmed and lidded urn decorated with palm leaves on lower half and a decorated banding. A draped cloth over the shoulders is taken down to the plinth. Inscribed centre top in sepia ink "70".

?William/John Paty.

77. Wove paper. 167 × 246. Ink, grey wash and Chinese ink. The same as No. 76 above but the parts in grey wash in No. 76 are in Chinese ink here. Draughtsmanship is poorer. Signed "Henry Wood" bottom right. Inscribed in pencil top left. "UI" Top right. "II". Bottom left. "8.0–3.4." and bottom right. "6–2.4".

Henry Wood.

78

78. Wove paper. Cut out. 95 × 176. Ink, grey wash and Chinese ink. Vertical oval, white memorial slab on black background rectangle. Simple base mould and eared and segmental base with eye in a sun-burst oval. Above, a cornice and a black double-curved "pyramid" on which a short plinth and a stemmed, banded and lidded urn with palm leaves around the lower section and with a mourning cloth draped around. The same design as No. 72 above.

Henry Wood.

79. Laid paper. 188 × 255. Ink, grey wash and watercolour. Vertical rectangular memorial slab with shouldered segmental top edge. A background of coloured marble at sides and top with two circular paterae at top R and L. Consol brackets at top R and L with a suspension of thick oak leaves. Below, a podium over memorial slab and background on a full cornice onto plain brackets at sides and an eared stepped and segmental white marble base. Above, a cornice and a grey Gothic-arched background on which a wide, curve-sided plinth with coloured heraldic badge with reed/acanthus-leaved supporters. Finished with a cornice

on which a stemmed broad urn with a domed lid with a flambeau handle. Lower body of urn has a palm-leaf fan. Rim of urn supports a draped cloth. Pencil inscription. Lower centre. "£45 guineas." (sic.).

Thomas Paty and Sons.

80. Laid paper. Cut out to shape of Gothic arch around monument. 123 × 233. A repeat of No.79 above except that the grey washed Gothic "pyramid" is omitted, although the Gothic-arch shape of the cut paper is nearly in the same position. The only other variation is in the design of the heraldic badge and its supporters which, in this case, are a pair of draped-leaf swags fixed to little paterae.

Thomas Paty and Sons.

81

81. Laid paper. 188 × 262. Ink, grey wash and watercolour and Chinese ink. A repeat of No. 68, except that the pyramid here is drawn in black and the background to the memorial slab is shown as coloured marble. The drawings are both by the same hand, probably William's, but there are actually two monuments of this design in St Michael's Church, one dedicated to William Keats, dated 1797 and so by William, and the other is to Patty Rigge dated 1786 and so by Thomas Paty and Sons.

Probably William Paty.

82. Laid paper. 166 × 240. Ink, grey wash and watercolour. A variant of No.s 74 and 75 without the flanking consol brackets and drapes, but with the marble background eared at the top, with a differently shaped cornice and without the top Gothic arched background slab.

Thomas Paty and Sons

83

83. Cream card. Cut out. Ink line. A rough ink drawing of neo-classical character. A rectangular memorial slab with a pair of thick pilaster strips and a base mould of similar size. The pilasters have a staff and twined serpent motif (medical). Above, a blocked cornice with dentils on which is roughed out a military achievement of a tall stemmed, banded and lidded urn with bold angled handles taken from shoulder to lid, surrounded by four flags on spears gathered to the base of the urn and under them, on either side, cannons, one facing beligerently outwards and the other, inwards; a plumed helmet, a laurel wreath and the hilt of a sword. The body of the urn bears the name "Edward". The whole design is contained within a rectangular form cut to a broad pyramid with gabled top.

This is a rough, ideas drawing but it lacks the sensitivity of No. 69.

Probably Henry Wood.

84

84. Laid paper. 185 × 292. Ink, grey wash. Rectangular memorial slab with shouldered, segmental top edge flanked by pilaster strips in marble with a moulding to define a "capital" of an oval patera. The moulding supported on a fan of acanthus leaves which carries a drape of four leaves down the pilaster. Below, a base moulding on a plinth to the pilasters and the memorial slab. Below it an eared and double curved marble base finishing to a curved bracket at the centre and plain brackets each side under the pilasters. Above, a classical cornice and a curve-sided large plinth on it with heraldic badge with ribbon-tied palm-leaf supporters. Above it another cornice on which a tall stemmed and lidded ovoid urn with top of oval body and fan of palm leaves and below this a knotted and draped mourning cloth.

Thomas Paty and Sons.

85

85. Laid paper. 215 × 292. (Only 133 is visible of the width as this drawing is lapped by drawings No. 84 and 86.) Ink, grey wash and watercolour. A vertical oval memorial slab on a coloured marble background which continues into the tympanum of a baroque, broken pediment: decorated with a ribbon tied in a bow and tassled, suspending a cloth which drapes right and left to lap onto the top of the oval memorial and taken up near to the top corners of the backing where it is knotted and draped, giving a grand baroque feel. Below, the marble backing is eared at the base and has a pair of circular patera decorated with leaved pendants. On a plain plinth onto a base mould and below, a segment-shaped base, flanked by triglyphs and plain brackets. Base decorated at the centre with a pair of crossed and flaming torches, tied with ribbon. Above, the broken pediment which has ears to contain a narrow strip of frieze with arcading and grand consol brackets and leaved drapes, below. On top of the pediment is a stemmed and lidded boat-shaped urn with handles and another draped cloth. The conical lid is grooved and the lower section of the body of the urn is decorated with palm leaves. On either side of the pediment are stemmed and lidded long ovoid urns with palm leaves on the lower half. Is almost identical to No. 54 except for the flanking pots.

Thomas Paty.

86. Laid paper. 187 × 292. Ink and grey wash. A repeat of

the design of No.s 79 and 80 above with grey marble backing and with a handsome cherub's head with extended wings on the base. Inscribed No. 2 at top centre.

Thomas Paty and Sons.

MONUMENTS WITH FIGURES OR PORTRAITS

87

87. Laid paper. 215 × 290. Ink, grey wash and watercolour. Memorial slab in S-shaped casket form with shaped coloured marble side strips. Below, a simple base moulding and a pair of triglyphs under the corners of the casket flanked with profiled plain brackets and, between the triglyphs, a shouldered and segmental base. The triglyphs have leaved fan brackets below. Above, a capping with ovolo moulding and a tall coloured marble gabled pyramid over the casket on which stands a naked cherub who leans on a tall stemmed and conical lidded urn. He holds one end of a leaved swag which drapes around the body of the urn. The cherub looks mournfully out to the right. Above, a heraldic badge with palm supports and a mailed-fist achievement. To left and right, sitting on the capping of the casket and outside the pyramid, a pair of tall stemmed and lidded urns. It resembles the monument in Babington Church to the Mompesson and Pacy families.

Thomas Paty. However, there is an edition of this monument in St Michael's Church, to Mary Stretton, dated 1794, by William Paty.

88

88. Laid paper. 195 × 238. Ink and grey wash. A vertical oval plaque with a standing naked, draped cherub who supports a heraldic shield with acanthus leaves. He points out the heraldry with his left hand. The oval stands on a foot onto a base mould. The background is a grey marble rectangle with eared base and pilaster strips in white veined marble on either side which have similar ears and capping moulds as capitals. Below the base mould, a pair of triglyphs at the outside enclose a curve-sided memorial slab onto a broad, central bracket. Above, a flat cornice and a white marble tympanum without any enclosing cornice. The draughtsmanship and the general character of this drawing are quite different.

Probably James Paty (3).

89. Laid paper. 140 × 228. Ink and grey wash. A shield-shaped memorial slab on a grey (slate) backing which is eared on either side and with a double curved base between them. Above, a beaded moulding and a cornice over it, on which sits a Gothic pointed arch in slate on

which "hangs" a white oval plaque with a profile portrait head. The plaque is pierced and threaded with a ribbon which is taken up to a rather ill-defined knotted cloth over. This drawing is also from a different hand.

Almost certainly James Paty (2).

90

90. Laid paper. 185 × 255. Ink and grey wash. A carved rectangular slab with a female figure in Greek dress, leaning on and pointing to the legend on a tall ovoid, stemmed and lidded urn whilst a child sits, reclining against the base of the urn, back to his mother. The carved slab is flanked by pilaster strips in marble and based with a plinth which is on a base moulding supported at the ends with plain brackets in front elevation, flanking a double curved base slab in marble which carries a heraldic shield. Above, a simple cap mould which carries a deep frieze which is, at the ends, a continuation of the pilaster strips in marble; in the centre is indicated the site of the memorial inscription. Above this, a cornice and, as with No. 88, a tympanum slab in marble, with no pediment. Inscribed centre top. "No.2" and top right in pencil "400". Draughtsmanship as in No. 88.

James Paty (3).

91

91. Detail paper. Cut to shape. 145 × 265. Ink line. A carefully drawn neo-classical design. A horizontal rectangular memorial slab flanked by pilasters with Greek acroteria at top and bottom of moulded recesses. Below, a simple base moulding and a square block decorated with a rosette and a horizontal base that matches the pilasters in width but decorated with a single central groove. Above, a Greek cornice and on it a plinth strip and a tall gabled pyramid. On the pyramid, a lady in a Greek dress holding an anchor looks out, disconsolate, and leans against a tall Greek urn on a decorated plinth. The drawing is signed "H. Wood, Sculptor".

Henry Wood.

92. Laid paper. 205 × 355. Torn at top right. Ink, grey wash and gouache. A horizontal rectangular memorial slab on a mustard yellow/orange background slab flanked with a pair of reversed consol brackets. Below, a heavy base mould, a pair of square blocks decorated with paterae at the outer edges, supported on leaved fan brackets. Between them, a base in a rich coloured marble which is curved, stepped and curved and finished at the lowest point with a fan bracket with leaves. The base marble has an edge frame in white and on the centre, a

cherub's head with spread wings. Above, a cornice and a plinth band on which sits a curve-sided "pyramid" of white and grey marble against which is a $\frac{3}{4}$-full face bust of a soldier in classical dress on a stand, surrounded with trophies, swords, flags and a trumpet. Above this a cornice capped with what looks like a curved, baroque pediment but which is in fact a pair of recumbent consol brackets on which, at the centre, is a flourish of acanthus leaves and reeds as a wreath that holds an acroterion at the top. This drawing is different from any other drawing in the book, but there is one other drawing that seems to be by the same hand, No. 28. There is a copy of this (No. 92) in Evercreech Parish Church, high up in the space below the clerestory on the south side of the nave, but it lacks the bust and pyramid and the trophies. Mr. Joseph Barker, to whom the monument was dedicated in 1715, seems not to have been a military man. The drawing is presumably the earliest in the book.
There is another edition of this monument, with the curved-sided pyramid but without the figure sculpture and without the winged cherub at the base, dedicated to George Musgrove obit. 1742, at Stogumber Church in Somerset, where they attribute it to Rysbrack.

James Paty (1).

92

93. Laid paper. 218 × 290. Ink and grey wash. Vertical rectangular memorial slab flanked by giant reversed consol brackets supporting a triglyph at each end and with two large guttae below a simple base mould. Between them an eared and double curved base. Above, a simple cornice on which is a grey gothic pointed pyramid with three oval portrait plaques with the profile heads of three men, the central one raised higher and slightly larger and suspended by a ribbon from a knotted pair of reversed grasses or reeds which droop to enclose all three portrait medallions. A faint pencil amendment suggests a baroque urn to the right of the backing.

James Paty (2).

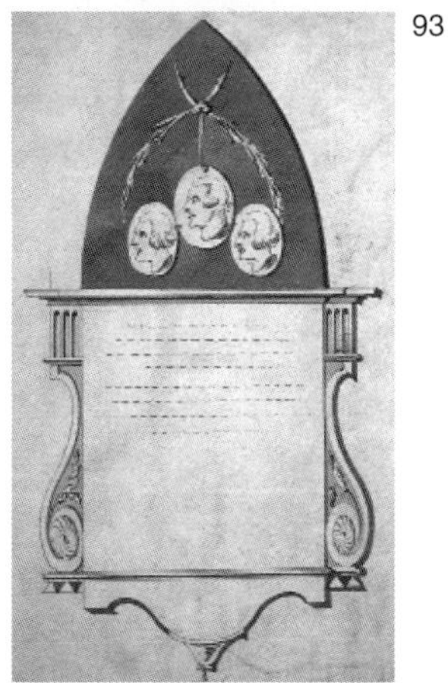

93

94. Wove paper. Watermark. 183 × 290. Ink, grey wash, watercolour. A large grey/blue Gothic arch-shaped marble slab on which is a rectangular memorial slab flanked by panelled pilaster strips and below, a base moulding with acanthus-leaved brackets supporting the pilasters and, between them, a framed, shouldered and segmental base member whose surface within the frame is reeded horizontally with an heraldic badge at its centre. Above, a neo-classical cornice on which is drawn in careful detail a kneeling, winged angel who holds a bulky stemmed, shouldered and lidded urn. The angel's head rests on the lid of the urn. She carries in her left

94

hand a long flaming torch and in her right hand, a garland of flowers and a drapery, against the side of the urn. A sprig of acanthus leaves lie at her feet. This is of unrecognisable but good quality draughtsmanship. The back of this is an advertisement for "Wm. Reeves and Son, Statuaries and C. 26, Charles Street, Bath. Monuments, Chimney pieces, Tombs &c &c". Part of an inscription is visible top right which includes part of a signature that might be "Henry Wood" and "Say about 6′0″ to 10′0″ high."

Wm. Reeves and Son (Bath) perhaps appropriated by Henry Wood.

MONUMENTS WITH HERALDIC BADGES OR OTHER DECORATIVE FEATURES

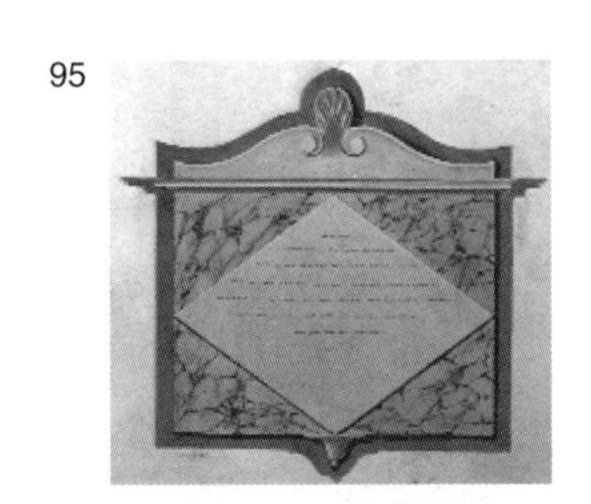
95

95, 96 & 97. Three cut out designs of simple memorials. 100 × 95, 105 × 158 and 100 × 95. Wove, laid and wove respectively. All ink, grey wash and water-colour.
95. A diamond shaped memorial slab on a coloured backing with a simple cornice and a double scroll-shaped top with a central acroterion.
96. A small simplified version of the standard Peter Fry design with no urn but an heraldic badge with palm leaf supporters at the top.
97. A repeat of No. 95 but with the diamond replaced by an unequal octagon, the background marble in greys only and with four paterae at the corners.

95 & 97 William Paty. 96 Thomas Paty and Sons.

98

98. Wove paper. Torn. 215 × 288. Ink, grey wash and Chinese ink. A rectangular memorial slab in a plain black edging with a brown edging beyond. Above, a neo-classical cornice and black and brown edgings continued. The memorial message is carefully drawn in full and reads:

In memory of
Mary the wife of Mr. John Goulter Jun.
of Petty France & daughter of
Nich. Morse Gent. of Ashmead House
who died 28th Dec, 1812
Aged 29 years.

Take Holy Earth all that my soul holds dear;
Take that best gift that heav'n so lately gave;
A Girl, our fondest wish (suppress the tear)
She did give birth; then bowed to take her leave,
and died. Does youth, does beauty read the line?
Does sympathetic fears their breasts alarm?
Speak, speak, dead Mary; Breath a strain divine;

Even from the grave thou shalt have power to charm.
Bid them be chast, be innocent like thee
Bid them in Duty's sphere as meekly move;
And, if's so fair, from Vanity as free;
As firm in friendship and as fond in love;
Tell them, tho' tis an awful thing to die
(Twas e'en to thee) yet the dread path once trod,
Heaven lifts its everlasting portals high
And bids the pure in heart, Behold Their God.

This agonised and agonising lament was presumably written by John Goulter and was recorded in marble by "I Wood ft. Bath" as is recorded at the bottom of the design. Could "I.Wood" be "Inricus" or some other invented latinization of Henry? A fragment of the original red book survives here.

Henry Wood?

99

99. Wove paper. 144 × 170. Ink, grey wash and watercolour and pencil. A long rectangular memorial slab with the legend indicated with pencil dashes. Flanked by blue marble pilaster strips divided into three by grooved mouldings. Below, a blocked base mould and a blue marble base with ears and a double curve. Three groups of guttae at each side and in the middle a heraldic shield at the centre. Above, a cornice with guttae as "capitals" over the pilasters. Above, a plinth strip and a blue marble "tympanum", its triangular form amended by three white discs which round out the angles. The result is similar to 1930s modernistic design.

Henry Wood.

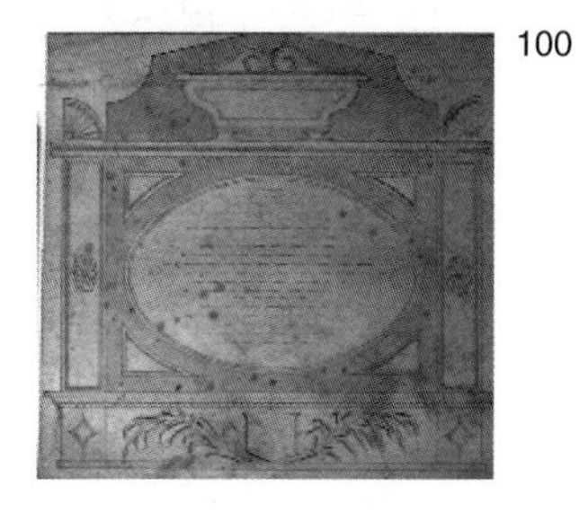
100

100. Wove paper. 197 × 182. Pencil and watercolour. A horizontal rectangular yellow background to an oval memorial slab which has triangular corner pieces and at each side, pilaster strips that are framed and have each an oval patera in the middle. Below, a base mould and a rectangular base strip stopped, each side with a block, decorated with curve-sided diamond shapes. Base has a heraldic shield in the centre with reed supporters filling the spaces at each side. Above, a reeded cornice and fan decorated acroteria at the ends and between them, a very low dark-yellow gabled background and on it a footed sarcophagus with double scroll-shaped top. A very neo-classical design. The use of pencil and yellow ochre wash is unusual. It is the only pencil and wash drawing in the book.

Henry Wood.

101. Wove paper. 145 × 140. Ink, grey wash and

watercolour. Some pencil construction lines. Horizontal rectangular memorial slab with segmental base and a blue marble backing at the sides and top which is double curved and which contains a heraldic shield. Below is a bracket base, signed H:Wood.

Henry Wood.

102

102. Laid paper. 140 × 190. Ink and grey wash. A vertical oval memorial slab on grey marble background with double curved and shouldered base and double curved top. Oval supported by a fan-leaved bracket at base and suspended from a ribbon from reed supporters to a shield. A simple and elegant design.

William Paty.

103. Laid paper. Ink, grey wash and watercolour. Vertical oval memorial slab onto a rectangular marble background with straight angle feet and two circular paterae at bottom, L and R. Ribbon, tied in a bow and with divided ends, over top of memorial slab. A narrow yellow marble plinth strip on base moulding and marble-eared, stepped and segmental curved base. Above, a small pair of consol brackets at sides and a cornice and plain blocked pediment enclosing a yellow marble tympanum.

James Paty (1) or James Paty (2).

104

104. Laid paper. 180 × 200. Ink, grey wash and watercolour. Horizontal rectangular memorial slab with segmental projection below in a coloured marble background, shaped to the memorial slab with a vase-shaped bracket with fan decoration, centre and guttae at right and left. Large consol brackets each side of the main slab with leaf drapes. Above, a straight cornice and above it a heraldic shield in a baroque flourish of acanthus leaves and reeds, all on a low grey marble background. Inscribed in pencil. Top left, "B.H." Bottom left. "3.10–3.8"

Thomas Paty.

105. Laid paper. 100 × 115. Ink and grey wash. A diamond-shaped memorial slab on a vertically reeded background rectangle which is itself on an oval grey background which cuts through the corners of the rectangle to appear at the sides and the bottom but does not appear at the top because masked with a cornice and a tympanum of similar grey colour. There is a shield on the centre of the tympanum. A crude design, crudely drawn.

Henry Wood.

106

106. Wove paper. 290 × 290. Ink, grey wash and Chinese ink. A horizontal oval memorial slab on a black background rectangle. Below, a simple base moulding and a narrow black base strip with ears each end and a bracket of guttae in the centre. Above, a crudely designed straight cornice with a low black sinuous curved top with a simple, empty heraldic badge. A narrow grey frame around the whole. Inscriptions. Top left "240" Middle left "3–2.82 Middle right. "3.9–3.3" Top right "563".

Henry Wood.

107

107. Laid paper with watermark. 174 × 249. Ink, grey wash and watercolour. Vertical rectangular memorial slab eared top and bottom and with circular paterae at the top. Coloured marble backing. Below, a base mould and a shaped marble base with ears and a segmental projection. Plain brackets in side elevation at the sides. Above, a pair of acanthus-leaved brackets in front elevation over the paterae support a broken pediment into which the coloured marble runs. In the tympanum a heraldic badge with acanthus-leaved supporters. Inscribed in ink "The underneath for the Rodbards". Not traced, but a similar monument in St Michael's Church is dedicated to Mary Daniels 1777.

Thomas Paty.

108

108. Laid paper. Cut out. 129 × 203. Ink, grey wash and watercolour. Vertical rectangular memorial slab with pilaster strips each side in coloured marble with cap mould and oval paterae at top. Below, a plinth slab and base moulding with tryglyphs under corner of memorial slab and plain side-elevation brackets outside. Between them, a shouldered and segmental coloured marble base. Above, a straight cornice and a coloured marble curved, stepped and curved background on which is a heraldic badge with a reed flourish support.

Thomas Paty.

109. Laid paper. Cut out. 125 × 175. Ink, grey wash and watercolour. Vertical rectangular memorial slab with top shouldered and with segmental projection. On coloured marble background which has consol brackets at the top, with leaf suspensions. Below, a base mould and a pair of acanthus-leaved brackets containing a plain rectangular base. Above, a straight cornice and an heraldic badge in a flourish of reeds on a triangular background with the outer corners cropped. This and No. 108 were clearly presented as an alternative pair. They were used in several monuments with the details freely transposed.

e.g. Conybeare monument. Bristol Cathedral, 1755. J. Tucker Woodward, 1758.

Thomas Paty.

110

111

112

110. Wove paper. 230 × 320. Ink, grey wash and watercolour. Square memorial slab with top projecting segment on shoulders, segment pressed to the top of a blue/grey marble backing which has a narrow framing strip and stands on a wide white, framed strip. Below, a base mould as a simple block which extends beyond the memorial and its framing to receive a tall ovoid, stemmed urn with tall neck but no lid, on each side. Below, a narrow base strip finishing either side in a square block under the urns. They contain a circular patera and are supported with a leafed bracket. The base between them is decorated with two cloths, knotted and draped. Above, the cornice consists of two slabs, the first dark and narrow and the upper a thicker light-coloured slab whose bulk is reduced by the edges of the face being framed. Above, a low pyramidal background for a large laurel wreath around a circular disc. Inscribed top left. "5–4 UX"

Henry Wood.

111. Laid paper. 225 × 215. Ink, grey wash and watercolour. Memorial slab in an ogee-sided shaped "casket" with grey marble shapes outside. Below, a simple base mould and two plain brackets either side of an eared, shouldered and segmental base. Above, a straight cornice and on it a large, framed bracket-shaped plinth in coloured marble, flanked by tall, ovoid, stemmed urns with narrow necks and flambeaux. On the plinth, a triangular pediment with a grey marble tympanum.

James Paty (1)? James Paty (2)?

112. Laid paper. 150 × 282. Ink, grey wash and watercolour. A rectangular memorial slab with a double curved top on a plain grey marble backing flanked with large consol brackets with small bunches of oak leaves beneath each. Below, a simple base mould and a base of double curved, stepped and eared shape. Above, a cornice and on it a rather narrow, double curved "pyramid" of grey marble with a large heraldic shield supported with reeds or narrow acanthus leaves. L.H. bottom corner missing.

Thomas Paty.

113. Laid paper. 184 × 283. Ink and grey wash. Rectangular memorial slab with ears and segmental top

and with circular paterae at top R and L on a grey marble background which flows into the tympanum of a broken pediment, the bottom members of which are supported on acanthus-leaved brackets which support leaved swags. Below, a large curved cassone with a bold, gadrooned, double curved, moulded lid, which breaks onto the memorial slab. The gadrooned cassone is flanked with similarly shaped side strips and below, a plain base and plain brackets which read as feet to the cassone. Above, the broken pediment on which is a heraldic badge with flourish and an armoured arm. The badge, supported with oak leaf drapes on either side, is taken down to the corners of the pediment. A good, old-fashioned baroque design by a young Thomas Paty.

113

Thomas Paty.

114. Wove paper. 166 × 137. Ink, grey wash and Chinese ink. Horizontal rectangle memorial slab on a dark grey rectangular background with ears at the bottom. Above, a straight cornice supported at the ends with narrow, long brackets in front elevation. On it a middle grey narrow plinth. The bottom line of the scribbled legend appears to say “1801”. Inscriptions in pencil. Top left “AO al” Bottom left. “3.2–2.5”.

Henry Wood.

115

115. Laid paper. 143 × 190. Ink, grey wash and pencil. A pair of oval memorial slabs, tilted towards each other at the top, and almost touching at the centre of a grey (slate?) backing which has a twice-draped mourning cloth knotted high centre and draped R and L to touch tops of each slab and then taken to another knot each side, slightly lower than the central one, from which a drape touches the outer extremity of the tilted slabs. The two slabs are joined where they come close together at the centre with a (wedding?) ring from which is suspended a heraldic shield. Below, four guttae as a central bracket. Above, a straight cornice. On this, a pencil addition, rather roughly indicated, of a cherub’s head and wings enclosed by a pair of brackets to form a baroque S-curved pediment with a shell-like heraldic shield above. This rather advanced design is somewhat reduced by the pencil additions. This is a late design and, excluding the pencil, is better drawn and more scholarly than Mr Wood’s work usually was.

Probably James Paty (3).

116. Laid paper. 138 × 279. Ink, grey wash and watercolour. Vertical rectangular memorial slab with pilasters at sides with three capped flutes and a cap

mould and a raised "capital". Below, a simple base moulding. A plain bracket in side elevation at each side and an eared and double curved base finished at centre with a plain, curved bracket. Above, a straight cornice on which is a grey marble curve-sided and gabled pyramid decorated with an heraldic badge with reed or narrow acanthus-leaved supporters. Above it a pair of reed swags draped down over the badge.

Thomas Paty.

117

117. Laid paper. Two tears on left. 182 × 245. Ink, grey wash and watercolour. Square memorial slab with coloured marble pilaster strips with cap mouldings which define the capitals above. Below, a plinth strip and a base moulding. Grey marble, eared, stepped and segmental base between plain brackets. Above, a straight cornice and a curve-sided grey marble pyramid with decurved, stepped and curved gable at the top. On it is a leafed swag tied with ribbon, central, high, looped to outside of pyramid and draped down following the outside of the pyramid for some distance. Below the swag, a baroque shield and surround. A rather dirty drawing and difficult to read. There is a slightly tentative feel about it although, as usual with Thomas Paty, the draughtsmanship is meticulous.

Perhaps early Thomas Paty.

118

118. Laid paper. Cut out. 115 × 195. Ink, grey wash and watercolour. Vertical oval memorial slab on rectangular coloured marble backing, with ears and circular paterae at the top. Below, a base moulding and rectangular base with ears and flanked with plain brackets. Above, a straight cornice and a curve-sided plinth open to a broken pediment at top with an heraldic shield and reed supporters and an achievement of a raised arm with spear, going into the tympanum.

Thomas Paty.

119. Laid paper. Cut out. Tear, top left. 123 × 195. Ink, grey wash and watercolour. Vertical rectangle memorial slab with shouldered, segmental base projection on coloured marble background with base extension to match. Above, a straight cornice and a shield with acanthus leaves and raised arm and spear achievement. Leaf swags from top of shield to cornice enclose a light grey washed background.

Thomas Paty.

120. Laid paper (writing paper?). Watermark. Folded. 205 × 300. Ink, grey wash and watercolour. Vertical

rectangular memorial slab with shoulders and segmental projection at base and coloured marble background with segmental projection to match. Above, a straight cornice and a coloured marble curved, stepped and semi-circular background, containing a pair of wings holding a crucifix. Inscribed in sepia ink. “Letters of the inscription $1\frac{1}{4}$ each. A monument of this design may be executed from £10 : 10 : 0–12 or 14 according to the size.” Vague pencil dimensions are also indicated.

120

Thomas Paty? James Paty (2)?

121. Laid paper. Cut out. 115 × 205. Ink, grey wash and Chinese ink. Vertical oval memorial slab on black background with ears top and bottom and with oval paterae at the top. Below, a simple base mould and another pair of oval paterae on black background panels enclosing a base member curved into an extended base with a broad central bracket. Above, a straight cornice and a double curve-topped black “pyramid” with a shield and reed supporters with a pair of wings and an arrowhead as achievement. A coarse, non-Paty drawing.

Henry Wood?

122

122. Wove paper. 200 × 275. Sepia ink and wash. Vertical rectangular memorial slab with pilaster strips in marble each side with cap moulds. Below, a plinth strip in marble, a base mould and simple brackets with eared base between, also marbled. Above, a full triangular pediment with marbled tympanum. Above, a tall marble pyramid with gabled top. On it, on top of the pediment, is a stemmed, boat-shaped flaming lamp. Inscribed “No. 1.”

Probably James Paty (1).

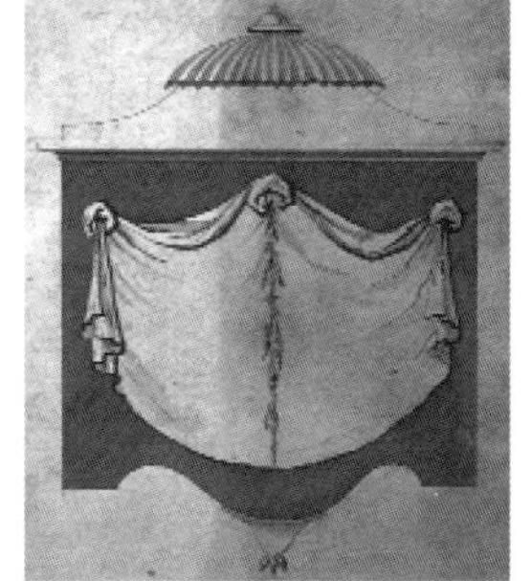
123

123. Laid paper. 173 × 234. Ink and grey wash. Memorial slab as a draped cloth tied centre and at sides with the central knot producing blood stains(?) down the centre which divides the slab in two. The bottom of the slab is a large segment of a circle to the sides where it meets the sides which are contained by draped, gathered ends of the cloth below the outer knots. The cloth is also draped at the top between the knots. All this is on a light grey background which is finished at the base with a sinuous curve between shoulders. Above, a straight cornice on which is a curved plain plinth capped with a broad, shallow fan-shaped dome with a domical knop above. There is a family resemblance both in design character and draughtsmanship to No. 115.

James Paty (3)?

124

124. Wove paper. 174 × 250. Ink, grey wash and watercolour. The paper outside the drawing of the monument is colour-washed a light purple/blue. Vertical oval memorial slab pierced and tied with bowed ribbon to coloured marble background which is eared at the base and has a pair of consol brackets at the top. Below, a narrow plinth strip and a base moulding and an eared and segmental shaped base in grey marble. Above, a straight cornice and the tympanum only of a pediment in coloured marble. This detail, particularly, suggests James Paty (2).

James Paty (2).

ARCHITECTURAL DRAWINGS & DETAILS

125

125. Laid paper. Central fold and a tear up the bottom 40mm of it. 305 × 236. Ink and grey wash. A carefully drawn and rendered architectural elevation of a civic building. It is a three-bay, two-storey building with the middle bay set forward and pedimented. The pediment carries a coat of arms that identifies it as a proposal for the rebuilding of the Merchants' Hall in King Street. This two-storey structure can be identified as for an adjacent site in Marsh Street that, in the event, did not come fully into the Merchants' Hall use until late in the nineteenth century when it was developed as an "elegant Committee room" after the demolition of the Treasurer's House in 1871. The drawing shows, at ground floor level, a central semi-circular-headed doorway in a rusticated wall. It has a projecting keystone and ten voussoirs and is flanked with a window on each side in the outer bays, which have segmental heads and five voussoirs. The rusticated wall is set on a low plinth and capped with a plain projecting string course, into which the main keystone dies. Above it a cill course, on which the upper floor windows sit. The central window is Venetian with Tuscan columns, an architrave, frieze, cornice and a semi-circular architrave over the central unit. Above the outer pilasters are two large circular paterae with swags of leaves draped over them. The centre bay is further decorated with long and short quoins, rusticated blocks above the cill course. The outer windows stand on projecting cills and carry architraves and an outer plain member which is the same width as a slender bracket which supports a triangular pediment over. The main cornice over the outer bays is completed with a balustraded parapet, stopped at the outer side with a solid corner which forms a podium for a stemmed and lidded tall urn with a prominent arcaded band. On the inner side, a similar podium actually runs into the top of the main pediment but provides the support for a second

urn. At the top of the main pediment is another, larger and grander urn which has no lid or middle band, but is draped and knotted. The tympanum of the pediment has the coat of arms of the Society of Merchant Venturers with its supporters of a mermaid on the left and Neptune on the right.
Apart from a little overstatement – it might have been better if the rustic quoins at first floor had been left off – this is an essay in eighteenth-century Palladian architecture and must be by Thomas Paty with William, still full of his London experiences, offering Adamesque paterae to the Merchants on his father's behalf, in the mid-1770s. The building eventually erected on this part of the site in 1871 was a coarse and heavy Victorian interpretation of some of the elements of this design.

Thomas Paty, 1770–80, with William Paty.

126. Laid paper. 225 × 330. Pencil line. Plan of the main and the bedroom floors of an unidentified house. Probably a survey drawing, although alternative plans are indicated on part of the bedroom floor, which states "store and bedroom or two bedrooms" at one position. The draughtsmanship is workaday, if not rough, but the writing on the plans is William Paty's copperplate. The house plan is of a simple rectangle of four bays on the front. The ground floor plan (the upper drawing on the sheet) has an entrance door at the second bay from the right and a narrow entrance passage that runs through the house to the rear, passing the staircase to the right and a narrower passage to the left into the kitchen zone. There are two living rooms (dining room and parlour) and six working and storage rooms. Upstairs, (the lower plan) has five or six bedrooms, two or three with dressing rooms or store rooms attached, and a study/library with its own store room or strong room. The plans are uncompromisingly "ordinary" and make no suggestion that could be indicative of architectural or spatial significance.

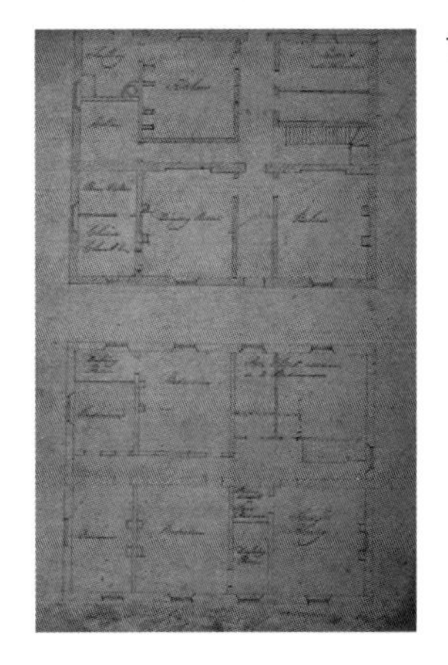
126

William Paty.

127. Wove paper. 292 × 455. Folded. All corners damaged. Etching with ink inscription. An etching of a memorial monument inscribed in ink, top right.

"Monument erecting at H—
to the memory of Lord Nelso—
by Mr. Thos. Wood 1806"
At the bottom, on the lowest step of the monument,
"Thos. Hardwicke Lond. inv et del. TW & JD
Hereford. Sculp."

127

The monument comprises a massive Tuscan column on a laurel-leaf base. The cap has egg-and-dart mouldings on the cushion of the cap and has four anchors on the cardinal faces below it, linked with two looped rows of rope which also coils around the shafts of the anchors. Above the cap is a block plinth on which is an effigy of Nelson, inappropriately dressed as a Roman warrior, and wielding a sword and holding an anchor? He only just fits in under the top edge of the paper. At the base, the laurel-leaf moulding sits on a triple block base which sits on a shallow plinth onto the cornice over a massive podium of cubic form which has angled pilasters at each corner. Between the angled pilasters the square space is sculptured in bas-relief and, on the side shown in the drawing, appears to be a depiction of the Battle of Trafalgar, above a "Glory" of an anchor, ensigns and swords. The face of the pilasters are also decorated with a vertical motif entwined with laurel leaves. The podium has a classical base and cornice and the whole is set on three steps. The monument stands in Hereford, on the Castle Bailey but Nelson, bare-chested and in Roman armoured shorts, gave way to an urn.
Thomas Wood was, presumably, a relation of Henry Wood's, perhaps his father or a brother.

Thomas Hardwicke.

128

128. Laid paper. 305 × 237. Ink, grey wash and watercolour. A beautifully drawn and rendered elevation, plan and side elevation of a fireplace, labelled in William Paty's hand "drawing room". Probably $\frac{1}{8}$th full size. At this scale, the fireplace opening is 3′6″ high and 3′10″ wide and the whole is 4′8″ high and 6′6″ wide. The surround consists of a red marble arcaded band in a white background with a beaded (long and two short) inner member and an egg-and-dart outer member plus cavetto moulding with square framed corner pieces with square paterae. Above, a frieze of two green marble plaques, carved with swags of roses and ribbons on each side of a central white marble plaque, uncarved and decorated with a row of guttae below. Outside this, a pair of grotesque pilasters formed as an elongated bracket which starts above a narrowed yellow ochre base and is in white marble with a green central inset which widens towards the top and which is stopped with a green block at the same level as and of the same depth as the paterae corners of the fireplace opening. Draped cloths are looped from bows at the centre top. Above the green block, a short curved and narrowing continuation of the column rises across the frieze to an Ionic capital with a draped wreath between the volutes. The capital rests immediately underneath the first moulding of the

modillioned cornice which is the mantlepiece. This steps out over the pilasters. This bold, positively Mannerist piece is nevertheless late in date and is certainly by William Paty at his best.

William Paty.

129

129. Wove paper. Ink, grey wash and watercolour. A handsome, simple fireplace design at a scale of 1″ to 1′0″. Fireplace opening 3′4″ high by 3′8″ wide. A narrow white nib around the opening and a 2″ wide blue marble surround and a 5″ wide plain pilaster strip and top of golden yellow (sienna) marble on a white base and with white square corner pieces with square paterae. A plain white unmoulded mantleshelf, perhaps $1\frac{1}{4}$″ thick. Outer edges of the pilaster strips have a narrow strip of blue marble. The whole is very simple, plain and elegant. Drawing shows the fireplace in its room setting with moulded skirting and dado rail in grey. Inscription; top right £12.0.10.″

William Paty.

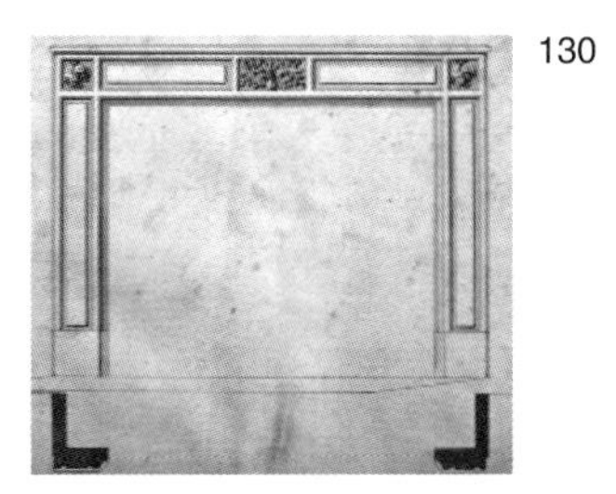
130

130. Wove paper. 269 × 234. Ink and grey wash. Elevation and plan of a neo-classical fireplace which has a scale marked of $1\frac{1}{2}$″ to 1′0″. ($\frac{1}{8}$th full size). Fireplace opening of 3′4″ high by 4′0″ wide. A 1″ grey margin round opening and then the main surround about 8″ wide arranged as a single framed panel at each side, a square frame with circular paterae at corners and a pair of framed panels and a central carved panel at the top. The plain panels have a raised centre and the carved central one has a tall, bulbous vase with flowers and leaves. The framing is chamfered. On top the mantlepiece hardly projects, has a straight vertical face and a top, curved chamfer. The plan shows the whole fireplace projecting nearly a foot from the wall.

William Paty?

131

131. Laid paper. 268 × 202. Ink and grey wash. An elegant standard Adam fireplace (timber and composition or wood carved) drawn at 1″ to 1′0″. 3′8″ square opening. A moulded strip and a 6″ white marble surround. An 8″ wide pilaster strip on a base. On it a pilaster, tapered from top, which is framed and carries garlands of acanthus leaves and ribbons. Above, a double moulding with acanthus decoration and then an 8″ deep frieze decorated with a broad, stemmed, lidded and curl-handled urn from which acanthus-leaved garlands reach out to clustered garlands in $2\frac{1}{2}$ groups each side before meeting the oval paterae above the pilasters on each side. Above, another narrow moulding and another

narrow frieze of alternating strips of arcaded niches with rosettes underneath the cornice (mantlepiece). The topmost ovolo moulding of the mantle is carved with egg-and-dart. This is a very elegant drawing.

Certainly William Paty.

132

132. Wove paper. 243 × 305. Ink and grey wash. An elegant fireplace that might have been intended in marble or in wood, but more likely marble. Scale, 1″ to 1′.0″. Same opening size and first surround as No. 131, then a pair of Corinthian columns that may be intended as free standing which have a single row of acanthus leaves in the Greek taste. On top a pair of narrow mouldings close together, reading as a reduced architrave before a wide frieze of two looped acanthus rings around oval patterae. Between them, a carved central plaque with a recumbent classic figure, who twists to carve into the trunk of a tree against which he had been leaning. Behind him is a landscape. He wears a laurel wreath or a hat like Mercury's. Above the columns in the space of the frieze, a pair of oval paterae on a rectangular block. Above this, a classical cornice as the mantlepiece. Drawn by the same hand as No. 131 and at the same time.

William Paty.

133. Wove paper? 210 × 178. Ink and grey wash and some red wash. A rather tentative Gothick design for a fireplace. Has a measuring line indicating its scale as 1″ to 1′0″. A plan in red wash indicates that the jambs of the opening are in the form of a five-sided figure, which, if made in the round, would be octagonal. A slender column is attached to each angle which finishes at the bottom with pear-shaped bases and above, with the same shapes, where they support a frieze band cut into with rectangular cusp-ended slots. Above this is a deep hollowed-out moulding, following the octagonal form of the base and after being interrupted by a stop mould, this continues into a deeply coved cornice, which again follows the octagonal form beneath it. It is completed with a sloping top and a step up to form an octagonal plinth, or rather, what would be octagonal if it were continued. The base of the coved cornice immediately above the stop moulding is scooped out in a repeating pattern to form a decorative band below the mantlepiece. A very shallow Gothic arch springs from the capitals of the collonettes across the fireplace opening, but there is not enough room and the arch touches the coved cornice at the centre of the span, making for a very weak appearance. The arch has a simple roll moulding edge, decorated with cusp shapes or half florets. Inscribed in

pencil, top right, "Statuary; £40.0.", perhaps referring to a proposal for statues to stand on the top plinths, although none is indicated. This is the only Gothick drawing in the book. Not even Henry Wood offers anything like it. Thomas Paty certainly built in Gothick from time to time and although this drawing is more timid than would usually be expected from him, it is a careful drawing as his drawings always are. I suggest that this is indeed the only known drawing in the Gothick taste by Thomas Paty.

Thomas Paty.

134

134. Laid paper 307 × 128. Ink and grey wash with red wash. Perhaps $1\frac{1}{2}''$ to a foot or $\frac{1}{8}$th full size. Firèplace opening 3′4″ wide by 3′2″ high. Narrow white surround and a cyma-recta moulding. Pilaster strip with ribbon and leaves pendant. Above it a moulded cap and oval paterae in rectangles with a frieze between them with a carved plaque at the centre. The frieze is of two loops of leaf-garland tied with ribbons and a vertical garland each side. The carved plaque is a delightful drawing of a lady making a sacrifice, accompanied by four female attendands/musicians. The plaque is tall enough to interrupt the lowest part of the modillioned cornice/mantelpiece. The fireplace opening has been rendered in a rich, deep grey-black which has then been carefully rubbed. Superimposed on the drawing is a full size detail plan of a pilaster which does not seem to belong to this design. It is rendered in a purple red but has been carefully handled so that the rendered parts do not interfere too much with the underlying drawing. For instance, it is stopped at the plaque so that the detail drawing of the classical figures does not have the wash over it.

Thomas Paty or William Paty.

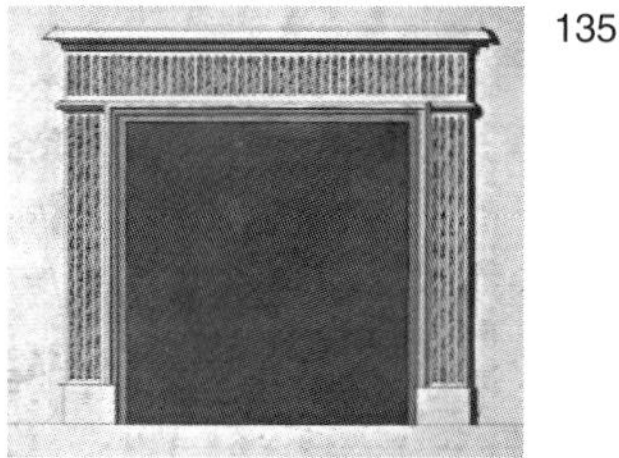
135

135. Laid paper. Watermark. 246 × 197. Ink, grey wash and watercolour. 1″ to 1′0″. Opening, 3′4″ wide by 3′6″ high. A narrow grey surround and a moulding onto a pilaster strip and lintel strip of white marble with inset arched vertical strips in green veined marble. A white marble mantlepiece with half-round and stepped edge. An elegant, very simple design.

William Paty.

136. Laid paper. 305 × 234. Ink and grey wash. Has a dimension line that shows it as $1\frac{1}{2}''$ to a foot or $\frac{1}{8}$th full size. Opening is inscribed in pencil as 4′0″ × 3′10″. Pilasters and lintel are of the same moulding with double steps to a 6″-wide white slab with a carved inset

136

of laurel leaves in bundles, the leaves pointing downwards on the pilasters and outwards on the lintel from a central point of crossed ribbons. Laurel-leaf decoration is stopped at the corners where a corner piece is decorated with four laurel leaves crossed. A simple and only very narrowly projecting mantelpiece has a hollow moulding above a vertical. Inscribed in ink, top right "No. 17". and in pencil on the fireplace opening "4′0″ and ″ ″3.10".

Thomas Paty or William Paty.

137

137. Laid paper. 292 × 234. Line dimension showing it to be $1\frac{1}{2}''$ to a foot. Ink, grey wash and pink wash. Watermark "Whatman". A bold, "modern" fireplace design. A simple architrave surround of roll moulding edge, plain frieze and ovolo frame against a 5″ quarter-circle of a Roman Doric fluted column. On top, a 6″ deep frieze with Greek leaf motifs. The frieze follows the shape of the quarter columns as does the mantel-piece over, which is an ovolo and a cyma-recta with a marble slab over.

William Paty.

138

138. Wove paper. Cut out. 190 × 222. Ink, sepia ink, grey wash and watercolour. A white memorial slab of horizontal rectangular shape but with cloth drapes, bows and ribbons at top and sides and black marble background. Pilasters of framed panelled form and simple moulded cap. Below, an edged base band with blocked ends and a double curved base with large fan at centre and small fans under the pilasters. A cornice and a plinth strip on which stands a blue marble backing with large segmental top. On this a memorial casket on legs and with a broad, reeded lid. On either side, a narrow v-shaped urn with flaming top.

Henry Wood.

Index

Entries in **bold** relate to illustrations